Sex, God's Creative Gift

Human Sexuality Revealed in Biblical Teaching

Vickrey Dougherty

Winston-Derek Publishers, Inc.
Pennywell Drive—P.O. Box 90883
Nashville, TN 37209

PUBLISHED BY WINSTON-DEREK PUBLISHERS, INC.
Nashville, Tennessee 37205

Library of Congress Catalog Card No: 88-50766
ISBN: 1-55523-155-1

Printed in the United States of America

Dedication

*To my parents, Emmet and Polley Dougherty,
who by precept and example, instilled in me
the sacredness of sex as a gift of our Creator.*

*To Anna, my beloved wife, who has shared
with me her beautiful sexuality for fifty years,
and who has supported me in this undertaking
with self-giving love.*

Acknowledgments

This book could not have been written without the help of many people.

To the Covina United Methodist Church youth and parents, who listened to the outline before I commenced writing and encouraged me to proceed.

To Dorothy Stumbo and Ruth Kermode, who first read a rough draft of my manuscript and encouraged me to continue with it.

To Rev. Ehrhardt Lang, whose theological insights and helpful suggestions prodded my continuing research.

To Ruby MacDonald, whose loving and professional critique of the whole manuscript helped me with changes that have made the whole book more interesting and understandable to all who read it.

To Brenda Hall, educational assistant at Arroyo Grande United Methodist Church, who read the completed manuscript and encouraged me to make changes that would be helpful to parents.

To William Gallagher, my loyal son-in-law, who has spent most of his professional life as an elementary school principal, for valuable suggestions about changes in school curriculum.

To Dr. Norman E. Tullis, M.D., who read the section dealing with venereal disease and made helpful recommendations.

To Rev. Everett L. Taylor for reading a late draft of this manuscript and making very helpful suggestions from a professional viewpoint.

To our grandson, Terry Withers, who read a late version, shared it with four of his friends, and made valuable recommendations from the perspective of young adults.

To Jeannie Aschenbrenner, mother of teen-age children, who read the manuscript and made useful suggestions from a parent's perspective.

To Ronald Gibbons who read a late copy of the manuscript and made several helpful suggestions.

To friends and fellow pilgrims along the way whose prayerful support helped keep me at the task. I gratefully acknowledge the assistance of all these in bringing this project to completion.

Contents

Foreward

I wish fervently that this book had been written when I was young, and that it had been read by my parents, pastors, and teachers. I had the feeling that since the mysterious subject of sex was something adults dared not talk about openly, there must be something forbidden or bad about it. But the normal, God-given sex drive and concomitant interest in the opposite sex naturally fueled the fires and stimulated intense interest.

Discussion with my peers provided a vast amount of misinformation, and a consequent sense of guilt. Since the topic often dealt with innuendos, implying that there was something desirable but forbidden, and probably very wicked, about sex, the result was conflict and tension.

But that was long ago. Now the pendulum has swung far to the other side. In movies and television, unmarried couples casually fall into bed and indulge in a kind of compulsory orgy of recreational sex; but in the films no girl ever becomes pregnant, and no one gets venereal disease, much less AIDS. The implication is clear: total sexual freedom is the norm, and without negative consequences.

Vickrey Dougherty treats the subject with reality, in a biblical context. He presents human sexuality as a marvelously beneficial gift of God, and his biblical approach to the subject robs it of its negative, guilt-ridden aura. Sex becomes the gift of God, along with all our other drives and emotions, to be expressed appropriately.

In my counseling practice over a period of many years, I have encountered hundreds of people who could have been spared neurosis, heartache, and tragedy had they been exposed to *Sex, God's Creative Gift.* It is a splendid book.

Cecil G. Osborne, Ph.D., D.D.

Introduction

This book has gradually grown in my thinking as parents have come to me asking where and how to find the Christian teachings about human sexuality they were taught as children. I have finally become aware of a real need in the lives of many people whose minds are filled with confusion about their own beliefs. Our churches are filled with sincere, searching people, with their roots in Christian teachings about sexual beliefs and behavior, who find themselves trying to train their own children who are surrounded by a "new morality."

The sexual mores of contemporary society are in such sharp contrast with the teachings Christian parents received in their childhood that they seem wrong to many parents who are trying to raise children in the latter decades of the twentieth century. Many of these adults have only vague memories of what they were taught in Sunday school and in their homes when they were children. They do not have a clear understanding of what was taught, much less where one would look in the Bible to find such teachings.

Finally, I decided that I would search through the Bible to find all of the references I could about sexual teachings and sexual behavior. I was surprised to find a remarkable consistency in Biblical teaching from the beginning in Genesis to the Revelation of John.

This book is written for all persons who want to know what the Bible teaches about sex and its purpose in creating secure, healthy families. It also tries to give the reasons why these teachings are important to family survival.

In the back of the book, I have included a guide to

Biblical teachings regarding both constructive and destructive sexual behavior. I hope that this will prove helpful to all who want to know what the Bible has to tell us about human sexuality and where to find those teachings.

< **CHAPTER ONE** >

Losing Sight of the Creator's Purpose for Sex

Ruth was desperate when she came to see me. The evening before, when she returned home, her children had been startled by something strange in her voice.

When Ruth arrived in my office, she was obviously terrified. There was no hesitation—none of the small talk with which most people begin "feeling out" a counselor whom they have never seen before. Ruth sat down and began pouring out the story of her children's reaction to her voice the night before. She said, "I know I have a demon, a--a-and he's getting me again now. I feel him, he's got me by the throat." I heard terror in her voice, saw it in her eyes, and knew she was ready to "climb the wall."

I reached across the desk and laid my hand on hers, which she grasped desperately. I said, "Let's ask God for his help."

With that I began to pray a very positive prayer affirming God's power over all evil and his great love for all his children. I thanked our Lord that in his earthly life he had always been able to cast out demons. I affirmed my faith that he had the same power today that he demonstrated in Galilee. I thanked him for being in the room with us now and asked him to bring his healing to this dear child of his, and drive the demon out of her life.

As I prayed, I could feel her gradually relaxing her tenacious grip on my hand. I knew that her mind was opening to God's truth and her heart to his love. She was beginning to feel safe again.

I concluded my prayer with a reaffirmation of God's absolute power and an expression of gratitude for his unconditional love.

When the prayer ended, Ruth was calm enough to converse normally. My first question was, "When did you first become aware of this demon controlling you?" Her answer led straight to the root of her problem. "You know, it is strange, I can't understand it. When I'm in any man's arms I feel wonderful, but afterward, when I go home to my children, I feel awful and yesterday this demon got me."

I then asked her what her parents taught her about sex and how it was to be used. She said that her parents were devout Christians. Her father was a local preacher in a well-known denomination; as a matter of fact, she had called him just that morning for help. She told me of reading the Bible and of her early faith in God. I asked her if her present lifestyle was in harmony with her faith. She replied in the negative.

I said, "Then your demon is really guilt, isn't it?" She answered, "I guess you are right," and began weeping almost uncontrollably.

Ruth was a 35-year-old divorcee with a 12-year-old son and a 14-year-old daughter. Until a year before, when her husband left her for a younger woman, she had been very happy. The sexual relationship with her husband had been a very meaningful and satisfying part of her life with him. When her husband left, her world had collapsed, and she missed the sexual tryst almost more than anything else.

There were other divorcees where she worked— both men and women. They were finding sexual desires fulfilled with each other and encouraged her to try it. Because of her Christian belief that sex outside of marriage was wrong, she had resisted advances from men for several months, but eventually she succumbed.

Nonetheless, Ruth never did feel comfortable in her new lifestyle. It went against her early training, and it did not seem right. She was teaching her children that sex was a precious, holy gift to be saved for the mate they would some day find. Every time she came home from a night of revelry she felt ashamed. By the time she came to see me, she was being destroyed by her guilt.

Ruth is only one of millions of people who have been raised in the Christian faith, but who have drifted away from that teaching. They live in a world where many of their friends practice a life of complete sexual freedom. Most of these friends are nice people, good workers, kind to others, and do not get into trouble with the law. For these multitudes with their roots in Judeo-Christian training and their bodies in a society whose sexual lifestyle is like that of the ancient Canaanites, there is confusion of mind and torture of spirit. Like Ruth, they find themselves torn between their beliefs and the way of life practiced by their neighbors.

A Century of Fantastic Change

Why are many people confused about proper sexual behavior? We live in a century of change. Within the last one hundred years, the automobile has replaced the horse and buggy. Man has progressed from the first wobbly flight at Kitty Hawk, North Carolina, in 1903, to walking on the moon in 1969. Telephone, radio, and television have become parts of everyday life.

At the beginning of this century, most people

accepted the authority of the Bible and Judeo-Christian values as guidelines for human behavior. This was true of the majority of people, both inside and outside the church. Probably the reason for those outside the church having this basic philosophy was that public school reading exercises were largely based on the classics. Works by authors such as Longfellow, Lowell, Tennyson, Milton, Shakespeare, and others whose writings were filled with Biblical allusions were read by most elementary and high school children. With this system, every child was exposed to, and to some extent his values were shaped by, Judeo-Christian morality. According to this belief, love for one's neighbor was second only to love for God.

Much of this has changed, however. Today, public school education usually tries to avoid any reference to Judeo-Christian morality. In its place, the educational system teaches humanistic good will, premised on man's ability to improve his destiny through keen observation, knowledge, self assertiveness, and natural progress. As a rule, it is only where the teachers themselves are Christians that Christian values come through to the children; whereas in the last decade of the nineteenth century, the regular curriculum itself, along with established community mores, made it difficult *not* to be exposed to these values.

In Biblical teaching there is a Creator who plans and maintains the whole universe. To this Creator all human beings are responsible. He commands us to love Him supremely and to love our neighbors as ourselves. Children were taught that the person who obeys God's laws, loves his neighbor, and works hard will have a good life. Beyond this life, there is eternal life and continuing development with God — a reward of eternal happiness which he has planned for all who learn to live by Divine principles and love for one another. There is also eternal suffering and punishment for those who reject God's reign and live by their own selfish desires.

On the other hand, in the early part of this century, we began teaching evolution in our schools. This theory emphasizes that the universe came into being by chance, and life was accidental. There is no Creator. Man's origin is not in God, but in a lower species of life. People are not children of God, but descendants of early primates. It is true that many Christians have said of evolution, "We believe that this is the way God did it." Yet most public schools do not mention, much less teach, what some Christians call "Theistic Evolution." According to the doctrine of evolution taught in most public schools, improvement and development in life does not come about by Divine plan, but by mutation and/or accident, and the inheritance of acquired characteristics. The universe came from nowhere and is going nowhere; the human species has developed gradually from more primitive types; humans have the most developed life and civilization of any species. This life is all, there is no future life such as "heaven" or "hell."

The rewards of life are what we can make for ourselves. Since there is nothing beyond this life, we must work for the best we can get out of the present moment. Heaven and hell are now. If we are lucky and know the right people, we will have success and prosperity. If we are unlucky, our circumstances will be modest to poor. Success depends on our brains and our ability to exploit life and get to the top ahead of our peers.

This fundamental philosophy—that life began by chance and develops by accident and is basically physical with nothing beyond—has profoundly altered our behavior toward each other. For this reason, many people reject divine law and expect nothing beyond this life. They pursue wealth, pleasure, and fun with zealous abandon and disregard for the welfare of others.

The conflict in people's thinking has resulted in great confusion. Many people have no goals other than to satisfy their cravings and urges. They want to find as much pleasure as possible. Perhaps this has brought about what we have called, "the now generation." Their reasoning seems to be quite logical. "If there is nothing beyond then I must get everything now. Failing this, I'm robbed of what life has to offer."

A Time of Confusion

Great changes in science, education, and communication have forced Christians to re-think and often reinterpret many passages of the Bible. Writers of the Bible lived and wrote in a time when most people thought that the world was flat and the sun orbited the earth. For example, the psalmist describes the sun as running a race across the sky. (Psa. 19:5-6). It would never have occurred to the writer that the sun was stationary and the earth was rotating. And that was not important to his song about the wonder of God's world anyway. People of his time believed that God and heaven were above the earth and hell was below. They couldn't imagine that earth was a rotating sphere, and what is above us at noon is below us at midnight. In our time, more of us think of heaven as total acceptance of the reign of God, who is everywhere. To us, God is the Creator of a universe more vast than our grandparents ever dreamed possible.

Since we have been forced, by what we have learned, to reinterpret parts of the Bible, people naturally have begun to question all Bible teaching. This questioning has caused some people to doubt Biblical truth. However, for many of us, searching and questioning has strengthened our faith in the accuracy and reliability of the great insights and teachings of scripture. We know that God is our final hope and authority. We believe that he loves us because we are his children. Even though we are sinners, Jesus gave his life for us. "God was in Christ, reconciling the world to himself." (II Cor. 5:19)* We know also that we must learn to love and value one another as God loves and values us. This is truth.

The Failure of Science and Education

We have now become aware of the limitations of science and education. In our generation, science and education have created a world where all mankind lives in fear of instant annihilation. Consequently, we have an alarming increase in teenage suicides, for many young people who live under the shadow of the mushroom cloud find it difficult to work for a future that may not exist. The prophecy of Jesus of Nazareth about "Men fainting with fear and foreboding of what is coming on the world" (Luke 21:26) has been fulfilled in our generation.

We have learned that neither science nor education are panaceas. They are only tools. In the hands of good persons, these tools are used to bless all people. In the hands of greedy, self-seeking pleasure lovers, these tools are used to increase the power of those who possess them over those who lack them. When it comes to "how" we shall use our great learning and vast technology, we have discovered that both education and science are morally bankrupt.

Hence, the great principle of the Bible which reminds us that we must value the Creator-God more than we value anything else needs to be taken seriously again. Another Biblical commandment which tells us to value (love) our neighbor as we value ourselves is daily growing in importance and relevance.

*Except as otherwise noted, all Biblical quotations are from the Revised Standard Version.

Along with these changes, we are beginning to question the vast upheaval in sexual attitudes and practices which has accompanied the technological revolution of the past forty years. We do know that in spite of the advances in education and science, our divorce rate has continued to climb with alarming speed. Children growing up in homes with both natural parents are a minority in many communities. We know that our children are less secure today than they were at the turn of the century or any time in our national history. It appears that our generation has lost sight of the Creator's purpose for sex.

The Bible Speaks Openly and Frankly About Sex

When there is so much insecurity and disaster in the American family, it may help to take a fresh look at the Bible and its teachings about the purposes and uses of sex. Many of us have never thought of looking in the Bible for answers to sexual problems. Moreover, some of us have found that church people often shun the mention of sex. Many of them still feel the hush-hush attitude of the Victorian past, which has done great damage to Christian people. Turning to the Bible, we find that it speaks with great frankness about sexual behavior in human beings. Does this surprise you? It amazes most people.

The Bible treats sex as a gift from our Creator. It also tells of an early method of birth control. (Gen. 38:9) It speaks of both fidelity and infidelity. There are reports of sexual abuse as well as sexual fulfillment. There are accounts of prostitutes, homosexuality, adultery, fornication, and incest. Husbands and wives are told not to deny each other sexual fulfillment except on brief occasions and for good reasons. Spouses are to love and care for each other as Christ loved the church and gave his life for it. Consider the Song of Solomon if you doubt that God's Word can treat this erotic subject with dignity and beauty. We find throughout the Bible both constructive and destructive uses of sex.

My search through the Scriptures has made me realize that there is nothing new about the sexual revolution of the twentieth century. It is only new to us; however, every facet of the "new" sexual freedom of our time has been tried, discarded, and tried again by people who lived millenniums ago. From their experiments with differing sexual lifestyles, they learned what was constructive and what was destructive.

History Offers Valuable Lessons

I believe that there is much that we can learn from the experiences of others who were confronted with the same problems we face. We do not need to try all of their experiments over again if we learn from history the results that they obtained.

In this book I call sex *God's Creative Gift* for several reasons.

First, sex serves to create a life-long bond of unity and love in body and spirit between husband and wife. It was and is designed by the Creator-God to enrich the marriage covenant with pleasure, mutual thrill and satisfaction, and a union which grows more precious to both mates as long as life lasts.

Second, through the sexual love of husband and wife comes children. Thus sex assists in the development of a home and family full of loving, caring, sacrificing, nurturing people who support, serve, and help one another throughout their lives.

Third, when mates have said hot words in anger or hurt or betrayed one another, and in suffering have repented and forgiven one another, sex is the holy gift of God that adds his seal of blessing to penitence and forgiveness and restores them to new life in both body and spirit.

It is my plan to study the development of the monogamous family, beginning with God's covenant with Abraham. We will learn that the Hebrew people not only had ways of worship and beliefs that differed from their Gentile neighbors, they also had very different lifestyles and values; their understanding of human sexuality also contrasted with that of their neighbors.

We will also study the teachings of Jesus and his disciples about human sexual behavior. We will discover the kind of families produced in societies where there was sexual freedom as well as those which developed where there were clearly defined guidelines governing sexual behavior. *We will learn about the value given to persons by each of these different modes of human behavior.*

For all who want to learn basic Biblical teaching about human sexual behavior, and why, and where in the Bible to find it, this book is written for you.

CHAPTER TWO

*A*braham and the Hebrews

We begin our study of the Judeo-Christian understanding of human sexuality with the story of Abraham and his descendants, the Hebrews. Abraham, whose original name was Abram, heard the call of God to leave his home and country. He was directed into the land of Canaan.

God appeared to Abram after he arrived in Canaan and told him that if he would keep His laws and commandments, He would make a great people of his descendants. By this people, "All nations of the earth shall bless themselves." (Gen. 18:18) Such a wonderful promise filled Abram with both excitement and hope.

Abram needed this renewal of hope desperately. To him, life seemed bleak indeed, because even though he had amassed great wealth, he still had no heir. Sarai, now in her seventies, and Abram, in his eighties, had totally lost hope of having children. They had both been suffering deeply because of Sarai's barrenness.

We cannot quite realize the depth of suffering which this problem brought to them until we understand that according to their theology, a man's immortality was in his male children. A man who died without a son was dead forever. This was the end. So how could God's promise that Abram would be the father of a great nation possibly be fulfilled?

We can see the depth of their agony when Sarai, believing that she was standing in the way of God's promise that from Abram would come a great nation, finally devised a plan. In selfless devotion to her husband, but with a heavy heart, she gave her Egyptian maid, Hagar, to Abram, saying, "Maybe we can have seed by her." This was her human solution to the problem of barrenness. No doubt, it was the answer to barrenness often used by the Canaanites among whom they were living.

Abram accepted this plan, because he, too, did not think he could fulfill God's promise to become the father of a great nation in any other way. This was a solution and at that time the *only human solution* to the problem of barrenness. So, Abram and Hagar had intercourse and a son, Ishmael, was born. Sarai's plan to produce a child had worked, but it also brought discord between her and Hagar, and the conflict became so great that Hagar ran away. She was met in the wilderness by an angel of God, who heard her prayer and told her to go back to Sarai. Hagar obeyed, but the relationship deteriorated until finally, when Ishmael was about fourteen, he and his mother left the family for good. (Gen. 21: 9,10,14-21)

About this same time, the angel came again to Abram and renewed the covenant which God wanted to make with him. He was told to walk blamelessly before God, who would fulfill the covenant and make of him a great nation. Abram pleaded with God that Ishmael might be accepted as heir of the covenant. However, God refused to accept that human solution. God insisted that Abram keep his laws and walk in his ways, which meant trusting the Creator-God and being true to the law of fidelity between husband and wife. God said that the physical sign of this covenant would be circumcision, which would also be the symbol for all heirs in future generation.

The covenant with God involved a great change. This new beginning was so complete that Abram would henceforth be known as Abraham, and Sarai as Sarah. (Gen. 17) God would also fulfill his part of the covenant: Sarah would conceive and bear a son, to be named Isaac, who would be heir to the covenant. Through him and his descendants, God would make a great people. Sarah and Abraham both laughed at the idea of her becoming pregnant so late in life, but God fulfilled his part of the covenant, and in due time, Isaac was born. Through Isaac the covenant was passed to succeeding generations.

The task of leading persons whose upbringing was in polygamy to a monogamous lifestyle is most difficult. It took God a long time to accomplish this goal. Readers who are familiar with the Bible will be aware that Abraham even owned concubines by whom he had children. (Gen. 25:6) However, these sons were not heirs of the covenant. After Abraham entered the Divine Covenant and Isaac was born, he gave gifts to the sons of his concubines and sent them out of the area which Isaac was to inherit.

Before we leave the matter of God dealing with Abraham and designating his descendants as a covenant people, we need to think carefully about the sign of the covenant.

And God said to Abraham:

> As for you, you shall keep my covenant, you and your descendants after you throughout their generations. This is my covenant, which you shall keep, between me and you and your descendants after you:
>
> Every male among you shall be circumcised. You shall be circumcised in the flesh of your foreskins, and it shall be a sign of the covenant between me and you. He that is eight days old among you shall be circumcised; every male throughout your generations, whether born in your

house, or bought with your money from any foreigner who is not of your offspring, both he that is born in your house and he that is bought with your money shall be circumcised. So shall my covenant be in your flesh an everlasting covenant. Any uncircumcised male who is not circumcised in the flesh of his foreskin shall be cut off from his people; he has broken my covenant." (Gen. 17:9-14)

Why should God choose circumcision as the sign identifying his covenant people? If his only reason was to have his people marked so that they could be distinguished from the rest of humanity, God could have instructed them to cut off the bottom lobe of one of their ears. This would not have impaired their hearing, and it would have been a distinguishing mark. For that matter, any scar that would not be a handicap could have been placed on almost any part of the body. But God did not choose any of these more simple ways of marking his covenant people; instead he chose circumcision. Why this particular sign? It was a symbol and at that time had nothing to do with health—but God must have had some reason.

Perhaps the reason God chose to have the sign of his covenant placed on the major male sex organ was to remind Abraham and all of his descendants that they were to have a different understanding of human sexuality from that of their neighbors.

The children of the covenant would be reminded daily that sex was a holy gift from their Creator. It was to be used only in the sacred commitment of marriage. Here it would enrich the bond between husband and wife as long as they both lived. It would also enable them to have children created in God's image, and it was to support them in the difficult task of raising these children from infants to mature adults. Also, it would remind them that every life brought into the world through sex was holy and precious to them and to God.

Sex was to be a holy tryst, binding husband and wife together in a covenant that would bless them and every child born to them. Each child would not only be their special child, but would also be a son or daughter of the Creator-God. Each would therefore be treated with dignity, love, and respect all of the days of his or her life. Through this covenant which recognized every person as a precious child of the Creator, every nation would eventually be blessed.

Now, I cannot pretend to know what was in the mind of God. However, these thoughts fill me with wonder and excitement. Further, we do know that the Hebrews had a caring concern for people which no other nation possessed.

God also heard Abraham's plea for Ishmael and promised that he also would be the father of princes and peoples. But of him God said, "He shall be a wild ass of a man, his hand against every man and every man's hand against him; and he shall ever dwell against all his kinsmen." (Gen. 16:12) Here we see one of the first indications of a very basic rule. Most children born outside of marriage, or in marriages that are temporary, have very real problems in their human relationships. They have a distinct disadvantage in their ability to relate to other people. There are, thank God, exceptions to this rule, but it is, nonetheless, fundamentally true that children from relationships which are temporary—whether within or outside of marriage—tend to be capable of only temporary relationships themselves.

Eventually, Abraham showed concern for his nephew, Lot, who lived in the Jordan Valley community of Sodom. Abraham knew that this town was so wicked that God was about to destroy it. He therefore earnestly interceded with God to spare the city for Lot's sake, or to save Lot and his family.

God answered Abraham's prayers by sending two

angels to rescue Lot. When Lot's neighbors tried to commit homosexual rape against the angels, they were afflicted with blindness. (Gen. 19) Next morning the angels insisted that Lot, his wife, and two daughters leave. They headed for Zoar, but while they were still on the way, brimstone began to fall on Sodom. Lot's wife looked back and died.

Lot arrived near Zoar with his two daughters, and they lived in a cave in the hills. These two girls had lost their fiances in Sodom. But they wanted children, so they made their father drunk with wine, and each daughter became pregnant through incestuous intercourse with him. (Gen. 19: 1-37)

Abraham's intercession with God saved his nephew's life, but he was unable to save Lot's daughters from sexual lifestyles that were popular among the people of Sodom. So, even though Lot belonged to Abraham's family, his descendants could not be part of the covenant people.

It is important for us to be aware that God's covenant with Abraham involved the marriage relationship between him and Sarah. God absolutely refused to accept any other plan. Those who were to bless mankind and enrich all of the nations of the world would be the children of the covenant, which included devotion to God and absolute fidelity between husband and wife. Through children in caring, loving homes, where both father and mother are devout, loving and faithful to each other throughout life, the Creator-God blesses all people.

A Lofty Covenant — Difficult to Preserve

The covenant was never easy to maintain. Many Christians know that Jacob, the grandson of Abraham, had two wives. As a matter of fact, he had four wives because he sired children not only with Leah and Rachel (his two wives), but also with Rachel's maid Bilhah and Leah's maid Zilpah. However, this was not Jacob's first choice.

Jacob loved Rachel, Laban's younger daughter, and worked seven years for his beloved. But when he had finished his years of labor, his Uncle Laban tricked him. He told Jacob that in their country, it was against the law for the younger daughter to marry before her older sister, so he gave Jacob his older daughter, Leah, as his wife. But Jacob loved Rachel enough to work seven more years to obtain her. After he received his true love, they found that she was unable to conceive. Hence, she gave Jacob her maid "as his wife" and Jacob had two sons by her.

Although Leah already had four sons, she was jealous because Rachel had sons by her maid. So she insisted that Jacob take her maid, Zilpah, and bear children for her. After this, Rachel conceived and her first-born was Joseph. Later, she died giving birth to Benjamin.

However, the four wives brought jealousy and favoritism into the household. For instance, the first child of the favorite wife was given special treatment by his father. Discord and dissension followed, and finally culminated in the older brothers selling their younger brother Joseph to the Ishmaelites, who took him to Egypt and sold him as a slave. This story is contained in Genesis, Chapters 29 to 38. The various rivalries, jealousies, and sufferings of this family give powerful support to monogamous families. In later years most of the descendants of Jacob became committed to having only one wife.

A Slave Becomes Prime Minister

We glimpse the powerful effect of the covenant between God and Abraham when, after four generations, Joseph, and finally all of his family, went into Egypt. Joseph arrived as a slave. He was bought by

Potiphar, the captain of Pharoah's body guards. Joseph was a child of the Covenant and faithful in his commitment to the Creator-God, which also made him love his master as he loved himself. He did his work well and soon advanced to become overseer of Potiphar's entire household. (Gen. 39)

However, Joseph had other assets which soon created problems for him. He was a handsome young man and his good looks attracted the attention of Potiphar's wife. She believed that sex was an instinct through which it is permissible for a person to find pleasure with any consenting adult. Day after day she begged Joseph to have intercourse with her while Potiphar was away at work. But Joseph, an heir to the Covenant, had been circumcised when he was eight days old. He was therefore constantly reminded of the Covenant, which recognized sex as a sacred gift to be used exclusively in the bond of marriage to create and nurture children.

In spite of the continual temptations from Potiphar's wife, Joseph never forgot who he was. Finally, one day, overwhelmed by her lust, she grabbed Joseph by his coat and tried to force him to lie with her. Joseph broke away and ran out of the house. This so infuriated her that she accused him of attempted rape. Potiphar had Joseph thrown into prison. (Gen. 39:1-20)

Even in the Egyptian prison, God was faithful to his part of the Covenant and blessed Joseph. Soon God brought Joseph out of the dungeon and made him Prime Minister of Egypt. (Gen. 40-41) He was second only to Pharoah in political power. Through the next seven years, Joseph directed all the Egyptian preparations for the terrible famine that he had predicted would come. During the years of drought, Joseph administered the relief program for the whole country. It was during this time that Joseph's family came to Egypt, first to buy grain and later to live. In gratitude to Joseph, Pharoah gave them an allotment of good farm land in the Nile Delta.

Here we see a clear picture of two different attitudes toward sex. The heirs of the Divine Covenant believed in sex as a holy gift of the Creator-God, but the Egyptians used sex for pleasure wherever and however it could be found. The Hebrews had durable, supportive families whose children grew up in the love and security of homes that nothing but death could separate. The children grew into strong, loving, capable men and women, who, in turn, created stable families of their own; whereas the Egyptians usually did not produce strong families because their main focus in sex was pleasure, rather than commitment. (See Ex. 1:8-9)

If the Egyptians did not want a child, they either aborted or abandoned it following birth. After three or four generations, the Egyptians became alarmed because the heirs of God's Covenant were about to outnumber them in their own land. First, they made slaves of them all. But soon it appeared there would be too many slaves, and the Egyptians feared that the Hebrews would revolt and overthrow their masters. They then took measures to kill all male babies born to Hebrews. The female babies would make good slaves and also would bring great sexual pleasure to their masters.

God Provides Guidelines for His People

At this time in history, God began fulfilling his part of the Covenant and saved the life of Moses. He then called him to lead the people out of bondage and across the desert to the promised land. After God had helped the Hebrews escape from Egypt, midway in their journey, they camped for a long time near Mount Sinai. Here, God met Moses and helped him formulate the basic moral rules which would enable his Covenant people to develop a good society and a civilization that would be a blessing to the whole world. (Ex. 1-20)

The heart of these rules is the Ten Commandments, laws familiar to most of us. (Ex. 20: 1-17) Looking at them analytically, we discover that only the first two deal with our relationship to the Creator-God or to any gods at all. *The other eight are laws governing relationships between people.* A person must not use God's name in vain, swear falsely, or deceive his neighbor. He must not steal, kill, or bear false witness against his neighbor, or covet anything that is his neighbor's, or commit adultery. On the positive side, the Hebrews were to honor their father and mother so that they might live long upon the earth.

In Leviticus, Chapters 18-20, we find a much fuller account of the rules governing human behavior. We are also given the reason for these rules and told that God's Covenant people are to be different from others in their human lifestyles. Their behavior towards one another must not be like that of Egyptians or of the Canaanites, whose land God was going to give them.

God's message is very clear:

> And the Lord said to Moses, "Say to this people of Israel, I am the Lord your God. You shall not do as they do in the land of Canaan to which I am bringing you. You shall not walk in their statutes. You shall do my ordinances and keep my statutes and walk in them. I am the Lord your God. You shall therefore keep my statutes and my ordinances, by doing which a man shall live. I am the Lord." (Lev. 18:1-5)

Here, God, speaking through Moses, made it clear and specific that he is developing a people with a lifestyle different from the behavior patterns of these Gentile nations. It is interesting that most of this section in Leviticus, Chapters 18-20, deals with sexual behavior.

From these three chapters of Leviticus, we also learn about the practices of the Canaanite peoples:

> And you shall not walk in the customs of the nation which I am casting out before you; for they did all these things and therefore I abhorred them. (Lev. 20:23)

The Canaanites worshiped sex. They made it the center of their thinking and behavior. They too believed that sex was given primarily for their pleasure—pleasure without commitment. Sex literally possessed them so that they thought about nothing else.

Dr. Jacob Milgrom says:

> The pagan world of the ancient Near East worshiped and deified sex. It reserved the term 'holy ones' for its cult prostitutes. No wonder Israel is charged with an exacting code of family purity whose violation means death.[1]

These chapters of Leviticus make it clear that the peoples of the Near East, at the time of the Exodus, worshiped sex and believed that its purpose was pleasure. In these societies, sexual indulgence was usually found through heterosexual or homosexual relationships. If no cooperative or even uncooperative human was available, one could still find pleasure by copulating with an animal. Incest ravaged their families as it does our today. No wonder that strict laws, in these chapters, warn the Hebrews not to copy the sexual lifestyles of their neighbors!

These passages also make it clear that destructive sexual practices are more than personal sins between those who practice them. They are sins against the nature God created. They destroy the social fabric and

---

[1] *The Interpreter's One Volume Commentary on the Bible,* ed. Charles M. Laymon (New York: Abingdon, 1971) p. 79

poison the roots of civilization.

Dr. Nathaniel Micklem states clearly:

> The corruption of sexual morals is much more than a
> number of private and individual offenses against morali-
> ty; it 'defiles the land' so that the land vomits forth its
> inhabitants or, as we might say, adducing much historical
> evidence, it destroys a civilization and leads to national
> disaster.[2]

It was because of the very obvious decay and death of tribes and nations all around them in the Near East areas that the Hebrews, under the guidance of God, provided such harsh penalties for any of their people who practiced any of these sexual deviations. In nearly every situation, the penalty was death to both parties. In the case of rape, only the man was executed, unless the woman failed to cry out for help. (Deut. 22:22-29)

While the Israelites were encamped in the desert at Mt. Sinai, Moses, in deep communion with the Creator-God, used this time of relative quiet to try to prepare his people for the temptations they would face in the promised land. He provided them with guidelines to keep the Holy Covenant, which God had made with their ancestor Abraham. He reminded them that they were a chosen people, called out from all of the other peoples of the world. Their responsibility was to live according to the plans, and by the lifestyle, that God had outlined for the well-being of His human family.

Almost all Gentiles were ignorant of God and His plans for the happiness of His people. Only the Hebrews, through the insight and Covenant made between God and Abraham, understood God's holy purpose for human happiness. They were a "called-out" people whose task consisted of keeping God's Covenant. Through them, God would eventually

---

[2]Nolan B. Harmon, ed. *The Interpreter's Bible,* 12 vols. (New York: Abingdon, 1953), Vol. 2, p. 95

restore His whole Creation to the well-being and happiness He had planned for all his children from the beginning.

A Tough Assignment

However, the Hebrews no sooner came into the promised land than many of them copied the destructive ways and practices of the Canaanite peoples. For most of their history, life was a struggle which often erupted into warfare between those who believed in and obeyed Yahweh, the Creator-God, and those who deserted him and worshiped Baal, Molech, and other Gentile deities.

The commandments relating to sexual behavior were best observed by the hard-working poor. Those who had to struggle for survival were usually God-fearing people who possessed great reverence for Yahweh.

On the contrary, wealthy Hebrews often practiced polygamy. The Israelites finally appointed a king, which most of them believed would improve their military position with neighboring countries. Then most of their kings followed the custom of kings in the area and developed large harems. David was said to have many wives and concubines, while his son Solomon had a harem of one thousand women. (I Kings 11:3) This practice created all kinds of rivalries and jealousies among the children. Instead of having loving, caring families, both David's and Solomon's children often hated and plotted against each other.

David's practice of having sex with many women in his harem seemed to create lustful thoughts that, at least once, got him into major trouble. (II Sam. 11, 12) One afternoon as he was walking on the balcony of his palace, he saw Bathsheba bathing. David's mind was filled with lust, and he sent servants to Bathsheba's house and brought her to the palace and committed adultery with her. She was the wife of Uriah, a very loyal soldier in David's army.

As a result of this adultery, Bathsheba became pregnant. When she sent word of this to David, the king ordered that Uriah be returned to the palace to report on the progress of the war. David then told Uriah to go home and spend the night with his wife and return to him in the morning to take a message to his commander. However, Uriah, out of his loyalty to his buddies who were still on the battlefield, refused to go home but spent the night at the palace barracks instead. His refusal to go home for the night meant that there was no way that Bathsheba could later pretend to her husband that he was the father of her child.

Next morning, David sent a message to his commander by this loyal soldier, which ordered that Uriah be placed in a dangerous spot where he would be killed. Thus David resorted to murder in order to cover up his adultery. He then brought Bathsheba to the palace and made her the favored member of his harem.

However, David was unable to hide his sin from God. The prophet Nathan came to David and confronted him with his sin. When the king admitted his guilt, Nathan told him that, because he had rebelled against God, committed adultery and had Uriah murdered, God would cause evil to rise up against him in his own household.

Soon David's elder son, Amnon, got a crush on his own half sister, Tamar, who was very beautiful. (II Sam. 13) He tried to get her to go to bed with him, but she told him that such a relationship was wrong. She then offered to become his wife if he would ask their father for her. However, Amnon did not want a wife, he only wanted sex. So he grabbed his sister and raped her. Then he sent her away and refused to see her any more. Absalom, who was Tamar's full brother, avenged his sister's shame by having friends kill Amnon.

Then David's son Absalom rebelled against him, committed adultery with the king's concubines, and almost stole the throne from his father. David's commanders crushed the revolt and Absalom was killed.

So David's adultery affected his family. It brought about rebellion, rape, and murder among his children. David acknowledged his sin, repented, and God forgave him. But his penitence did not bring the loyal soldier Uriah back to life. Nor did it make any impression on David's sons Amnon and Absalom.

The Hebrews did not become a great and powerful nation who ruled over others, which is what most of them wanted. Instead, they were a servant people, preserving the good news of a holy, just and righteous God, for themselves and, eventually, their Gentile neighbors.

The thing that saved the Jews, and has preserved them as a special and identifiable people through all of the centuries, was that there has always been a remnant of the devout who kept God's laws. For this minority, sex was a sacred gift.

This holy remnant of the faithful, because of the presence and power of God within their families, has preserved the Hebrew people and made them a great blessing to all the world, just as God had promised Abraham. They have given the world some of its finest poets, scholars, scientists, statesmen, doctors, and musicians. Even Jesus, the Christ, was born and raised in a devout Jewish home.

The Jewish accomplishment and contributions to the world amaze us all the more when we realize that they have had national identity and independent statehood for only about four-and-one-half centuries. Their freedom began with Saul and David, and ended when the Babylonians conquered their country and carried them into captivity in 587 B.C. Except for the partial and temporary success of the Maccabees, the Jews did not have the benefit of an autonomous nation again until 1948, when the new state of Israel came into being.

Throughout history the greatest Jewish contributions to the world have come from the remnant of the devout, where faith was preserved in homes whose members revered God's laws. The Covenant understanding of family made life itself sacred and filled with meaning and purpose. It not only enabled the Jewish People to survive without a state, it also became leaven in most nations into which the Jews went. It brought about an awareness of the worth of persons far beyond the understanding of human values previously held by Gentile peoples. The worth and rights of persons as human beings grew in all areas where devout Jews went. The faithful took with them their concepts of God as holy and just, and followed lifestyles which preserved the family and produced children who grew to be courageous, just and kind.

We have taken this careful look at the Hebrews because the Creator-God was able to get the attention of Abraham more than that of any other person of his time. Because Abraham listened in obedience to God and tried to keep His laws, God was able to reveal His will and purposes for His children more clearly to him than any of his neighbors. Therefore, God singled out Abraham and his descendants for a special covenant.

As mentioned before, God promised Abraham that he would make of him and his heirs who kept the covenant a great people. Abraham promised, on his part, that he would obey God's laws, which involved keeping sacred the husband-wife relationship between him and Sarah. He accepted the physical sign of circumcision and, at ninety-nine years of age, had himself and all males in his household circumcised. This sign was the symbol of monotheism and changed lifestyle, in which sex was accepted as a holy gift from the Creator-God to be used exclusively for building the sacred marriage bond between husband and wife.

It is easy to see that this constructive view of sex and the family gives worth and dignity to each person. This is the *sine qua non* of all human civilization. Without this understanding of sex and family life, the value and dignity of persons soon begins to erode. Before long, dignity disappears.

CHAPTER THREE

Family Life at the Time of Jesus

Hebrew Dilemma: Obey God or Copy Neighbors

Life became a constant struggle after the Hebrews entered the promised land with clear guidelines to protect the family. At first they expected to exterminate all Canaanite people. The Israelites believed that if they could totally possess the land and purge it from the fertility cults and all of those who believed that sex was for pleasure without commitment, they would have complete security.

However, they could not accomplish this goal. Their "search and destroy" missions were a failure. They finally conquered most of the Canaanite people and took all of the best land for themselves. Still, pockets of subdued Canaanites lived in their midst. As mentioned earlier, Hebrews always faced the temptation to copy Gentile lifestyles and to worship Gentile deities. In times when the Israelites were true to the Holy Covenant, they prospered and life became quite secure. But when life became too easy, people forgot God's laws, turned to Gentile pleasures, lifestyles, and also to Gentile worship.

Ultimately the Jews suffered defeat. They lived as captives in Babylon for many years. When at last they returned to Palestine, even in their homeland, Gentiles ruled them. At the time of Christ, the Jews had been under Roman authority for more than a century. The Romans had conquered all of the known world west of

China and India.

We now want to look at family life in the Roman world at the time of Christ. We can better comprehend Jesus' teachings about marriage and the family if we understand the society in which he lived. First, let us consider family life in Greece.

Leader of World Culture

Greece, the center of education and learning for the civilized world, set the pattern for cultural life throughout the entire Roman Empire. With the exception of the Jews, most other people in Rome's domain desired Greek culture. Of course, few Jews would ever admit that Gentiles had any affect on them. However, it is easy for historians to see the definite impact of Greek culture on the Jews at the time of Jesus.

What was family life like in Greece?

Most classical scholars agree that Greek family life was a disaster. For example, when Jesus lived, most of the Near East treated women as slaves, and in Greece, the position of women enrages the modern mind. It is an affront to all people who believe in fairness.

The Greek matron lived in almost complete seclusion. She took care of household affairs, raised the children, and kept herself for her husband. She could never leave the house by herself. She could not even eat with the men of the household. Her husband expected absolute purity from her, but for himself, he demanded total sexual freedom. Instead of being frowned upon or considered wrong, promiscuous fornication and adultery were accepted as the normal way of life for all men.

Speaking of the Greek culture, Demosthenes said:

"We have courtesans for the sake of pleasure; we have concubines for the sake of daily co-habitation; we have wives for the purpose of having children legitimately, and of having a faithful guardian for all our household affairs."[1]

With this kind of marital inequity, there could be no happiness in the Greek family. Love did not exist. Lust and exploitation were the rule. Greece was the philosophic and societal leader of the Roman Empire; therefore, these Greek ideas about family life and male sexual freedom profoundly affected the lives and families of millions of people who lived in Rome's domain. Even Judea felt the pull of this lifestyle.

Disaster Overtakes the Roman Family

The real head and political center of the Empire was Rome itself. Here we find one of the most vivid illustrations in all of history regarding the impact of the "sex for pleasure" idea on the family life of a great and home-loving people.

In the early years of the Roman Republic, the home was precious. Great character developed in secure homes, which produced people who were loyal to both community and country.[2] Like an ever-flowing fountain, strong families created the qualities which supported a growing civilization. Unlike the Greeks, the Romans did not shut their women out of the main stream of life. They shared life fully with their husbands, and the husband was usually faithful to his wife.

There were indeed prostitutes, but to associate with them was shameful.[3] One Roman judge was assaulted in a house of ill-fame, but he refused to sue his opponent because to do so would have been to

[1] William Barclay, *The Gospel of Matthew*, Revi. Ed., Vol. 1 (Philadelphia: Westminster Press, 1975) pp. 153-155.

[2] Barclay, *The Letter to the Romans*, Rev. Ed. (Westminster, 1975) pp. 30-32.

[3] Barclay, *Gospel of Matthew*, pp. 156-157.

admit that he actually was in such a place.

Roman morality was so high that for the first five hundred years of the republic, there is not a single recorded divorce. But tragedy awaited the naive Romans.

Near the end of the third century, B.C., the government of Rome decided to conquer Greece. It had little trouble making subjects of the Greek people. In the next century a constant stream of occupation troops, returning home, brought Greek ideas of sexual freedom to Rome. With great speed, Hellenist immorality permeated nearly every part of Roman life. Divorce became common. The destruction of family life was catastrophic.

Lucius Seneca, the Roman philosopher, a contemporary of Christ, tells of women who were married to be divorced and divorced to be married, and on and on. Many men and women were married and divorced every year. One woman had eight husbands in five years.

With the lack of family commitment, the children who managed to escape the abortionist's art were often neglected or abused. Thus they learned to resent others and were against the establishment that had brought them into such evil conditions, where they were neglected instead of being loved and nurtured. The results of the demise of the Roman family were felt not only in the home, but in every area of Roman life. Community spirit disappeared and patriotism died. There was no purpose in living; nothing in either community or empire seemed worth living or dying for.

In this morass of addiction to sex for pleasure, without commitment, all that was great in Roman civilization died. Roman armies suffered no defeat, and the Roman Senate was neither ordered nor voted out of existence, yet hoards of stone-age people poured through Alpine passes, destroying everything in sight and taking what they wanted. They sacked and burned the cities. The decay of Roman character undermined all attempts to organize a coordinated or united resistance to the menace.

Thus, Rome fell because of the decay of human character brought about by the collapse of the Roman family. When Romans accepted the idea of sexual freedom as normal behavior, their doom was sealed.

Family Life Among God's Chosen People

We have looked at the family life of Greece and Rome. We now turn our attention to the Jewish family.

At the beginning of the first century of the Christian era, Jews were scattered throughout the Roman Empire. They even had synagogues in all of the principal cities. Even so, Jews of the dispersion often returned to their home land for celebrations such as Passover and Pentecost. It was inevitable that Gentile ethics and lifestyles would have a major impact of Jewish relationships and behavior. Therefore, we should not be surprised to find some Jewish Rabbis making a strenuous effort to greatly liberalize the Hebrew laws governing marriage and the family. As a result, divorce had become quite common among the Jews in the time when Jesus lived and taught.[4] Only when we realize what was happening to Jewish family life can we understand why the teachings of Jesus about divorce were so strict.

Ideally, the Jewish understanding of marriage was the world's highest. They believed that it was every man's duty to marry and raise children. This was so important that the only reason one might abstain from marriage or postpone it was to devote full time to the study of God's law. The duty to marry and raise children was so important that even the military could not

[4]Barclay, *Gospel of Matthew,* pp. 150-152

draft a recently married man.

> When a man is newly married, he is not to be drafted
> into military service or any other public duty. He is to be
> excused from duty for one year, so that he can stay at
> home and make his wife happy. (Deut. 24:5 TEV)

In all their teachings, the Jews abhorred divorce. No prophet makes this more clear than Malachi. We read these words:

> . . . You drown the Lord's altar with tears, weeping
> and wailing because he no longer accepts the offerings
> you bring him. You ask why he no longer accepts them. It
> is because he knows you have broken your promise to the
> wife you married when you were young. She was your
> partner, and you have broken your promise to her,
> although you promised before God that you would be
> faithful to her. What was his purpose in this? It was that
> you would have children who are truly God's people. So
> make sure that none of you breaks his promise to his
> wife. "I hate divorce," says the Lord God of Israel. "I hate it
> when one of you does such a cruel thing to his wife. Make
> sure that you do not break your promise to be faithful to
> your wife." (Mal. 2:13-16 TEV)

Malachi gives us the strongest statement against divorce to be found in the Old Testament. Apparently many Jews were forsaking their wives, when they got older, and were marrying young Gentile wives. The prophet condemns the desertion of a faithful wife in the strongest terms.

The Jews had the highest moral standards and put the greatest value on home and family of any people in the ancient world. The pathetic reality was, however, that practice fell far short of the goal.

One factor which damaged the whole marriage relationship for the Jews was their low concept of woman. Before the law, woman was a "thing." She was owned either by her father or her husband. She had no rights of her own. According to rabbinic law, a woman could be divorced against her will, but a man could only be divorced with his consent.[5]

To make this problem even worse, the law of divorce was quite simple in statement and very debatable in meaning. It simply stated: "When a man takes a wife and marries her, if then she finds no favor in his eyes because he has found some indecency in her, he writes her a bill of divorce and puts it in her hand and sends her out of his house." (Deut. 24:1)

There is no court hearing. All the man had to do to divorce the woman was to write: "This is from me your writ of divorce and letter of dismissal. You are free to marry whomsoever you wish." Then, in the presence of two witnesses, he would give her this note. That was the end. She had no recourse.

To the Jews the crux of the problem of divorce was in the interpretation of the phrase, "If he finds some uncleanness in her." Jewish lawyers were divided into two schools of thought regarding the meaning of this sentence. Rabbi Shammai and his followers insisted that "some indecency" meant unchastity and only unchastity. Thus, to them the only possible grounds for divorce was adultery or unchastity.

Another school of thought headed by Rabbi Hillel was liberal and defined "some indecency" in the widest possible way. They said that a man could divorce his wife if she put too much salt in his food or if she said unkind things about his parents when he was present. They allowed a man to divorce his wife if she was quarrelsome or if she spoke to other men in the streets. William Barclay says: "A certain Rabbi, Akiba, said that the phrase 'if she find no favor in his sight' meant that a man might divorce his wife if he found a woman whom he considered to be more attractive

5 Barclay, *The Gospel of Matthew,* p. 152.

than she."[6] Given the human trait of seeking the easy way and the quest for immediate rewards, it is plain to see which interpretation would be followed by most people. Divorce among the Jews had become so common when Jesus lived that many girls were refusing to be married. Many young women found life at home with pappa much better than marrying a man who would divorce them as soon as he saw a more attractive female.

I have given these descriptions of family life in Greece, Rome, and Judea so that we can gain a clearer understanding of the causes of the death of the Greco-Roman and Jewish civilizations. In the world in which Jesus lived, family life was demoralized. Indeed, this was the primary cause of the death of the Roman Empire and of the civilization built around it.

Our sociologists are convinced that no civilization can survive the collapse of the human family. At least we know that none of the early cultures were able to survive when the family was destroyed. Why should we expect it to be different now?

[6] Barclay, *The Gospel of Matthew*, p. 152.

CHAPTER FOUR

The Teachings of Jesus About Family and Sex

The Family of Jesus

Before considering Jesus' teachings on family and sex, I must tell you about his parents, Joseph and Mary. We naturally expect the teaching of Jesus about sex and the family to be profoundly influenced by the home in which he grew up. Both of his parents were devout Jews who committed themselves to Abraham's covenant. In their understanding, marriage was a holy covenant made by two people in the presence of God. This sacred, life-long commitment could be broken for no reason except unchastity or adultery.

Mary and Joseph belonged to the devout poor who longed for the coming of the Messiah, strictly kept the commandments of the Levitic law, and reverently kept in close communion with God. This deep reverence and daily contact with God enabled Him to reveal to Mary that she would be the mother of the long-promised Messiah. When Joseph first heard of Mary's pregnancy (which he undoubtedly learned about from her), it hurt him to the core. One of the reasons for Joseph's suffering and deep concern arose because he and Mary were betrothed when she told him she was pregnant. We can get a much better understanding of his pain when we realize that Jewish marriage was divided into three stages.[1]

---

[1] William Barclay, *The Gospel of Matthew,* Rev. ed. (Philadelphia: Westminster, 1975) Vol. 1, p. 18-19.

First came the engagement. This was either arranged by the parents or a professional matchmaker. The Jews considered marriage too vital a part of life to leave to the emotions of the persons involved. So every marriage was carefully thought through and evaluated by experienced parents or a person trained in matching qualities and character traits.

The second step was the betrothal. In this act, the couple themselves ratified the engagement, which had been made previously by others. At this time the engagement could be broken if the girl was unwilling to proceed with it. However, once they entered into betrothal, it was absolute and unbreakable except by death or adultery. Betrothal lasted for one year. It could only be terminated by divorce, even though during this year the couple had no conjugal rights. If the woman's fiance died during the year of betrothal, she was called "a virgin who is a widow." This seems strange to us, but it was common Jewish practice.

The Jewish reasoning about the year of betrothal seems to be this: If the couple had the kind of continence that enabled them to live in the same house (usually with the man's family) for a year without sexual intercourse, they knew that they could trust each other's fidelity throughout a lifetime of marriage. But if they did not have enough self-discipline to be faithful to each other for one year, while refraining from intercourse, it was better to end the betrothal with divorce before children arrived to be hurt by a break-up of the marriage. So the year of betrothal was a real test.

The third step was the marriage itself, a great celebration at the end of the year of betrothal.

Joseph and Mary were in the middle of their year of betrothal when Mary confided her pregnancy to him. He was keeping Mary a virgin. When she told him of her conception by the Holy Spirit, he was stunned. He knew well enough how a woman became pregnant. It hurt him to learn that the one he loved had not only been unfaithful to him but was lying to protect herself and her lover. Under the law (Lev. 20:10), both of those involved in adultery should be put to death.

However, in Joseph's agony over what he felt was Mary's betrayal and deception, because he was a devout man, he turned to God for guidance. God's angel convinced Joseph that Mary had told the truth and that he, Joseph, had been chosen to be the earthly father of the Messiah. Once Joseph understood God's plan, he devoted himself to it without reservation.

Joseph continued to keep in close touch with God, and as a result was given the strength to keep Mary a virgin until after the birth of Jesus. Matthew says, "When Joseph awoke from sleep, he did as the angel of the Lord commanded him; he took his wife, but knew her not until she had borne a son; and he called his name Jesus." (Matt. 1:24-25)

Joseph listened so intently for God's guidance that God could warn him of King Herod's murderous intention. Moreover, Joseph was committed to the safety of Jesus so that he obeyed God immediately and left Bethlehem, by night, for Egypt. Some men would have argued, but their was no argument from Joseph. His son's life was all that mattered. He obeyed God, went to Egypt, and stayed there until the death of Herod. Then he returned with his family to Nazareth.

In order to take a deeper look into the kind of home in which Jesus grew up, we need to get a better understanding of the Jewish plan of betrothal. We have learned that Jewish betrothals lasted for one year, and during that year the pair had all of the privileges of marriage except conjugal rights. The Jews knew the importance of common interests to marital harmony. They were also fully aware of the irritations that develop when persons from different families start putting their expectations together. They knew that harmony in their mutual relationship and the ability to cope with each other's differences, were vital skills for them to learn before children complicated their adjustments to each other.

They had a year in which to learn to love each other with caring, lasting devotion. They knew, too, that pleasure in sex was not adequate to produce emotional and spiritual harmony when bad tempers and personal selfishness are a constant source of irritation. They had a deep and abiding faith (reinforced by generations of experience since the days of Abraham) that, if there was mutual love and devotion between them as persons, males and females are so well designed physically by the Creator that sex will be a rewarding and fulfilling experience for both. Today there may be a need for correcting unwholesome or Victorian attitudes toward sex, but this can be accomplished with professional help. However, in those days, the Jews had no prudish attitudes toward sex.

The Teachings of Jesus Reflect His Home Training

Jesus saw a great contrast between the kind of home he came from and the shattered families which were so common among the Jews of his time. Throughout his entire ministry, we find two traits of Jesus that are outstanding: First, his compassion and forgiveness toward the victims of splintered families. Second, his sharpness and severity when speaking about the causes of family decay.

The primary cause of the destruction of the family grew out of sexual laxity and depravity. The penetration of Jewish life by the Gentile belief in sex for the pleasure of the moment was destroying many homes in Israel. Jesus gave strong support to those principles that strengthen the family.

Throughout his ministry, Jesus renewed and reinforced the Hebrew commandment against adultery:

> You have heard that it was said, "you shall not commit
> adultery." But I say to you that every one who looks at a
> woman lustfully has already committed adultery with her
> in his heart. If your right eye causes you to sin, pluck it
> out and throw it away; it is better that you lose one of
> your members than that your whole body be thrown into
> hell. And if your right hand causes you to sin, cut it off
> and throw it away; it is better that you lose one of your
> members than that your whole body go into hell. (Matt.
> 5:27-30)

Jesus not only reaffirmed the Hebrew commandment against the act of adultery but added that adultery begins in the thoughts of the mind and the lust of
the eye. He says that the impure thought and the lingering, lust-producing look must be excised before
they lead to the sinful act, which he insists begins in
the lustful mind and heart and then destroys the
whole body in hell.

Jesus definitely wanted to prevent the decay of the
family. He knew the destruction that came from
adopting loose attitudes toward sex . . . attitudes
which, as we have seen, were widely accepted
throughout the Roman Empire as well as among the
Jews of the first century.

The reason Jesus spoke so clearly about lustful
thoughts and why his disciples in the early church
were absolute in their condemnation of fornication[2]

---

[2]I will be using the words "adultery" and "fornication" in the rest of this book
because the New Testament uses them quite often. As I use them and as the
New Testament uses them, they have specific meanings. Though often confused
by people, they are not interchangeable.

The word "adultery" is a very specific term, referring to voluntary sexual intercourse between a married person and someone not his or her spouse. "Fornication" means voluntary sexual intercourse between unmarried persons or persons
not married to each other.

As I use these terms, "adultery" always refers to infidelity in marriage. "Fornication" refers to voluntary intercourse between unmarried persons.

lies in the kind of impact on fidelity such thoughts and actions bring to the one who embraces them.

What many people living in the first century did not see, Jesus clearly saw: that the mind which is trained in lust in early life will later be the mind controlling the behavior of the husband or wife. Eventually it will also be the mind that controls the father or mother of a family. This was the destructive power inherent in the ancient belief that sex between consenting adults was all right. It was even more disastrous when a teenager decided that sex was a good activity. *Jesus and the early church clearly recognized that lustful thinking and sexual intercourse before marriage are education for and training in adultery after marriage.*

What Jesus is saying in Matthew 5:27-30, and what the early Christian Church taught, is that the person who allows his mind to be filled with lust will lean toward repetitive sexual intercourse before marriage, and will often fall into adultery after marriage.

One of the clearest pictures we have of Jesus dealing with adultery is related by John:

> Early in the morning he came again to the temple; all the people came to him and he sat down and taught them. The scribes and the Pharisees brought a woman who had been caught in adultery, and placing her in their midst they said to him, "Teacher, this woman has been caught in the act of adultery. Now in the law Moses commanded us to stone such. What do you say about her?" This they said to test him, that they might have some charge to bring against him. Jesus bent down and wrote with his finger on the ground.
>
> And as they continued to ask him, he stood up and said to them, "Let him who is without sin among you be the first to throw a stone at her." And once more he bent down and wrote with his finger on the ground, but when they heard it, they went away one by one, beginning with the eldest, and Jesus was left alone with the woman standing before him.
>
> Jesus looked up and said to her, "Woman, where are

they? Has no one condemned you?" She said, "No one, Lord." And Jesus said, "Neither do I condemn you; go, and do not sin again." (John 8:1-11)

While it is true that many ancient manuscripts do not contain this passage, it is in keeping with the attitudes and teachings of Jesus on other occasions. It reveals his fairness, compassion, and firmness.

Several things become apparent in this account. First of all, we are impressed with the compassion of Jesus in stark contrast to the uncaring legalism of the Pharisees and Sadducees, who saw the woman not as a person but as an object to be used by them to trap Jesus. They were eager to use her for their own ends. However, they were not really interested in law enforcement and justice, because if she had been caught in the act of adultery, as they charged, there must have been a man involved also. But they had brought only the woman. Justice and real law enforcement would have demanded that the man be executed also. "If a man commits adultery with the wife of his neighbor, both the adulterer and the adulteress shall be put to death." (Lev. 20:10) But the Pharisees and Sadducees were condemning only the woman.

Jesus, aware of their hypocrisy and also of the terrified woman, bent down and wrote on the ground. The Pharisees and Sadducees believed they had Jesus in a trap. If he said, "Go ahead and stone her," he would be violating Roman law, for the Romans did not allow Jews to execute people. If Jesus said, "Forgive her," he would be in violation of the law of Moses and they would charge him with being disloyal to Jewish law. But Jesus surprised them when he said, "Let him that is without sin among you cast the first stone at her." With that, her accusers, convicted by their own consciences, began to leave.

Then Jesus began to deal with her as a person. We

must notice here that there are none of the questions about how she felt, or whether she really loved the person with whom she had sinned, which would be common practice in modern counseling. For Jesus, what she had done was *sin* and he was unequivocal at that point. The only feeling which she could possibly have, real enough to deal with, was her sense of shame and guilt. Jesus dealt with this clearly and forthrightly. He told her that he did not condemn her, but that she should "go and sin no more." In plain language, he told her to make a new start and to live a life free from lust and the sin that lust had caused.

From this passage we see the uncompromising position of Jesus, in which he identified with the Old Testament, that adultery was sin. He clearly called this woman's act a sin, granted her forgiveness, and told her not to repeat it. He gave her a chance for a new beginning. The conclusion we reach from this passage is that in the sight of Jesus, adultery is wrong, and it must be both forgiven and excised from one's life.

No passage in all of the gospels more clearly reveals the mind and thinking of Jesus about both fornication and adultery than a statement which is recorded by both Matthew and Mark. Jesus is explaining to his disciples what he meant in a confrontation he had with the Pharisees about what really defiles a person. He said to his followers:

> It is what comes out of a man that defiles him. For from inside, out of a man's heart, come evil thoughts, acts of fornication, of theft, murder, adultery, ruthless greed, and malice; fraud, indecency, envy, slander, arrogance, and folly; these evil things all come from inside, and they defile the man." (Mark 7:21-23 NEB. See also Matt. 15:15-20)

The Pharisees had accused Jesus' disciples of eating

without washing their hands in the ceremonial way. They thought that a person was made unclean by what entered his mouth. Jesus insisted that it is not what goes into the mouth that defiles a person. He said that what makes a person unclean is evil thinking in one's heart and mind, which comes out in words and actions that harm both the individual harboring them and others.

This is the most vivid place in the Gospels where Jesus specifically refers to fornication—sex between unmarried persons—as evil, though on numerous occasions, as we have seen, he refers to adultery as a sin. Here, however, he clearly describes sexual relations between unmarried persons as an evil which makes the persons unclean. This scripture reveals with unmistakable clarity the thinking of Jesus about sexual behavior with no commitment beyond the pleasure of the moment. In his thinking, fornication and adultery are in the same class with murder, theft, deceit, and slander. He calls all of these things evil. This makes very clear what Jesus expects the sexual behavior of his followers will be.

He said that marriage was a sacred commitment, designed by the Creator as a life-long relationship between a male and female who love and care for each other. He taught that they were to be faithful to each other throughout life. He said that we must expunge lust and lustful thoughts from our minds because impure behavior has its origin in impure thoughts.

Moreover, there is absolutely no wavering or equivocation in the teachings of Jesus about marriage; marriage is for the pure in heart and is designed by God as a life-long commitment. It is not an experiment which one tries for a while to see if it will work. It is a commitment which two lovers undertake, and grow with, through joy and sorrow, through good times and bad times, in sickness and in health until death parts them.

Marriage makes possible the highest development of character and fulfillment of personality, since neither party can run from his or her weaknesses just because the going gets hard. Both are to continue loving and growing toward perfection in a relationship and in the ability to give oneself completely to another, that God planned as the highest reward for all his children.

Jesus is consistent in his support of life-long marriage and sexual purity. Mark writes:

> The Pharisees came up and, in order to test him, asked, "Is it lawful for a man to divorce his wife?" He answered them, "What did Moses command you?" They said, "Moses allowed a man to write a certificate of divorce, and to put her away." But Jesus said to them, "For your hardness of heart he wrote you this commandment. But from the beginning of creation, God made them male and female. For this reason a man shall leave his father and mother and be joined to his wife, and the two shall become one. What therefore God has joined together, let not man put asunder. (Mark 10: 2-9)

(Parallel passages are recorded by all three synoptic gospel writers. See Matt. 19:3-12 and Luke 16:18)

The Pharisees, always enemies of Jesus, were trying to get him involved in one of their legal hassles. As we have seen, Rabbis of Jesus' time divided into very different schools of thought about divorce. Some were very strict; others allowed divorce for almost any reason.

These Pharisees tried to get Jesus to take one side or the other. He refused. Instead he told them that in God's plan, the intent was for a man and a woman to grow in their ability to love and help each other throughout life. He seemed to be saying that, because of hardness of heart and unwillingness of one or both spouses to repent and forgive and love, divorce might be allowed. This was the reason it was allowed by Moses. However, Jesus insisted that this was not the original plan and intention of God for any marriage.

Jesus is not talking about what may or must be done when worst comes to worst. He is emphasizing the Divine intent and and dream in the heart of God when he ordained marriage. That intent was that two people would love, help and give themselves for and to each other. When they failed and hurt each other, they would repent, forgive and restore each other to a new beginning. They would continue to grow toward more perfect personality. In character, each would become more Christ-like. Their love, support, self-sacrifice, and growth would become more precious to each as long as life lasts. This is the intent of God for all his children.

We conclude that the teachings of Jesus relating to sex and marriage emphasize great principles. They do not involve legalism. He taught that lust must be excised from one's mind and thoughts because fornication and adultery begin in one's thinking. He supported life-long marriage as the intention of God for all his children.

CHAPTER FIVE

Early Christian Teaching and Living

When we look at the teachings of the young Christian church about sex and the family, we find a pattern that is consistent with the teachings of our Lord. In fact, the writers of the New Testament are very specific about both the sanctity of marriage and the destructiveness of sex outside marriage.

Perhaps New Testament writers are even more specific than you would expect. The reason for this is that the young church soon moved beyond Jewish territory and into the Gentile world. Here there was almost no background or understanding of sex as a sacred and holy gift of God for the purpose of creating and nurturing children in loving, caring families. Nor was there any concept of the role of sex in bonding husband and wife to each other, enabling them to grow in unity and closeness.

Most of our information about the sexual teachings and practices of the early Christian church comes from the writings of Dr. Luke and the missionary to the Gentiles, Paul. However, there is enough material on this subject in Hebrews, Peter, Jude, and the Revelation of John to make the position of each of these writers completely clear.

The First Christian Conference

Nowhere in the New Testament is the young church's understanding of the divine purpose and plan for sex made more clear than in the account of the Jerusalem Conference, which is recorded in the 15th chapter of Acts. At the time of this event, the Christian Church had spread beyond Palestine, and under the missionary efforts of Paul, Silas, Barnabas, John Mark, and many less well-known Christians, it was making thousands of converts among the Gentiles throughout most of the Roman Empire.

Perhaps you will be surprised to learn that most Jewish synagogues, which were located in the cities of Gentile countries, had groups of Gentile worshippers in them! In fact, two different groups of Gentiles worshiped regularly in synagogues. The first, called Proselytes, actually converted to Judaism and kept all Jewish teachings including ceremonial law. The men of this group were circumcised according to Jewish custom. The second, a much larger group, called God-fearers, accepted Jewish belief in one God, but took no part in ceremonial laws, nor were their men circumcised. Many of these people listened and worshiped in every synagogue. It was from both of these groups that thousands became converts to the Christian Gospel.

Because of the conversion of many Gentiles and their entrance into Christian churches, a division developed among Christian teachers and apostles over how much of the Jewish law the Gentile converts to the Christian faith would be required to keep. Most of the Christian teachers were Jews, and without really thinking about it, they expected Gentile converts to convert to Judaism; they thought that Gentiles who accepted the Christian faith should be circumcised and keep all other parts of Jewish laws and rituals.

Hence the Jerusalem Conference was a battle between two different groups of Jewish Christians, while Gentiles, who were to be most affected by the outcome, were excluded. The conflict among Jewish disciples of Jesus greatly hindered the missionary efforts of all Christians who worked in the Gentile world, and it spread confusion among Gentile converts. For this reason, the leaders of the young church decided to call a conference in Jerusalem to deal with the problem. They wanted consistency not confusion.

In the meeting of church leaders assembled in Jerusalem, all points of view were first heard. Everyone had the opportunity to present his ideas and discuss them with others before a decision, to which there had to be common agreement, could be reached. Christian leaders from Palestine, as well as missionaries to Gentile countries, were heard. Peter related how the Holy Spirit guided him to the home of the Roman Centurion, Cornelius. He said that, when he was still speaking about Jesus to those present, the Holy Spirit came upon these uncircumcised Gentiles, just as He had first come upon the Jewish disciples on the day of Pentecost. This report of a personal experience helped the conference reach a consensus which all present felt was right and guided by the Spirit of God.

According to this decision, only four requirements would be made of Gentiles; this resolution was sent to all Gentile churches in the form of a letter. Two apostles from the Jerusalem Church, Judas and Silas, were sent to take the letter to the Gentile Christians.

> We, the apostles and elders, send greetings as brothers to our brothers of Gentile origin in Antioch, Syria, and Cilicia. Forasmuch as we have heard that some of our number, without any instructions from us, have disturbed you with their talk and unsettled your minds, we have resolved unanimously to send to you our chosen representatives with our well-beloved Barnabas and Paul, who have devoted themselves to the cause of our Lord Jesus Christ. We are therefore sending Judas (called Barsabbas) and Silas, who will themselves confirm this by word of mouth. It is the decision of the Holy Spirit, and our decision, to lay no further burden upon you beyond these essentials: you are to abstain from meat that has been

offered to idols, from blood, from anything that has been strangled, and from fornication. If you keep yourselves free from these things, you will be doing right. Farewell. (Acts 15:23-29 NEB)

These four requirements made genuine fellowship possible between Gentile and Jewish Christians in local congregations. In addition, they simplified the Jewish laws pertaining to eating and drinking. Eating meat which had been offered to an idol was deemed by the Jews an act of worship of that idol. Both Jews and Hebrew Christians considered this to be a violation of the first and second commandments: "Thou shalt have no other gods before me; thou shalt not make any graven image." (Ex. 20:3-4A KJV) The two requirements to avoid drinking blood or eating animals which had been strangled, which of course had the blood in them, was a concession to Jewish Christians. To Jews, the blood was the life, and therefore sacred.

The fourth requirement made of Gentile Christians demanded abstinence from fornication or unchastity. This was given for the protection of the families of Gentile Christians. Certainly, high morality in sexual matters was one of the factors of the Jewish religion which attracted Gentiles to Judaism in the first place. Therefore, this requirement would be gladly accepted by most Gentile converts as a joyous and wonderful transformation of their families. Living with this guideline would bring love, caring, joy, fellowship, and trust into each home; before conversion to Judaism and the Christian faith, there had been infidelity, quarreling, fighting, discord, and other ills that accompany casual sex. The Jews regarded these four requirements as commandments from the Creator of life. They believed that disaster and death would surely come if such laws were disobeyed. No sincere Jew could compromise on these points. Through the keeping of these four provisions, both Jews and Gentiles entered into the loving, caring fellowship of the Christian Church.

One of the greatest concerns of the Christian Church had been the many incidents of sex outside marriage as practiced by most pagans. The stark contrast between the young Christian churches with their happy, holy and joyous families and the unhappy, unfaithful, quarreling families in the world outside, became obvious to everyone—to the Christians themselves and to the pagans who coveted their lifestyle. No other single factor was more responsible for the rapid growth of the Christian faith than the strength and beauty of the Christian family.

To this point, in studying the teachings and practices of the young Christian church regarding sex and the family, I have used information from the first Christian Council meeting reported by Luke. Let us now look at other passages by different authors. We want to see if the position proclaimed by the leaders at the Jerusalem conference was also the accepted belief and practice of other writers of the New Testament who mention the subject of sex.

Paul Speaks Clearly About Sexual Behavior

Paul is a good person to listen to. It is probable that he knew life both as a married man and as a celibate missionary. While we know nothing about Paul's wife, he was most likely married before he became a Christian. It seems quite clear that he was a member of the Sanhedrin—the ruling Jewish Council—and we do know that no unmarried man could be a member of this council. William Barclay tells us that apostasy (forsaking the Jewish faith) was one of three conditions under which a Jewish woman could divorce her husband.[1] It therefore seems reasonable to conclude

---

[1] William Barclay, *The Gospel of Luke* (Philadelphia: Westminster: 1956), p. 219.

that either Paul's wife had died or, when he was converted to Christianity, she divorced him. Thus he became a celibate missionary, re-directing his sexual energies toward begetting new Christians and organizing churches in the service of our Lord. (I Cor. 7:8)

In the first chapter of Romans, Paul deals with the terrible depravity which had overtaken Roman life. Many families had been destroyed by lust and fornication. Living for the average citizen centered around sensual pleasures, and thus the divorces these vices produced were numerous, as I have mentioned. We must realize, however, that this was not only the situation of the average Roman family, but lust and sexual depravity reached to the highest leadership in the country. According to William Barclay, the Roman poet Juvenal, "Cites the incredible case of Agrippina, the empress herself, wife of Claudius, who at night used to leave the royal palace and go down to serve in a brothel for the sake of sheer, unsated lust."[2] This quotation from Juvenal makes it clear that Paul was not exaggerating regarding Roman immorality. Roman moralists were aware of the mess they were in and made more severe criticisms of their society than Paul did.

Paul contends that the wrath of God is constantly being revealed from heaven against all wickedness and that people who indulge in such shameless acts receive, in their own persons, the due penalty for their error. (Rom. 1:26-32) What Paul did not know, except by divine insight, we now know as a fact of history. Sexual and moral depravity utterly and totally destroyed Roman civilization. What no foreign general or army could ever accomplish—the destruction of Rome—was done by the Romans themselves through their sexual immorality.

[2]Barclay, *The Letter to the Romans*,, Rev. ed. (Westminster: 1956), p. 25

One of the reasons for Paul's eagerness to preach the gospel in Rome was because he knew that only the acceptance of the Good News of Jesus Christ could save Rome from disaster. Paul did get to Rome, but only as a prisoner. From his message and influence many wonderful conversions took place, but too few Romans accepted the Christian lifestyle to save Roman civilization, so it perished, but history records that the Christian Church grew in power and strength and became a blessing to ever-increasing numbers of people.

The Sex Capital of the Roman Empire

Nowhere in all of the writings of Paul is sexual immorality and lust more clearly and explicitly dealt with than in his first letter to the Corinthians. Corinth was a city of commerce, a bustling city, located at the narrowest part of the isthmus which connects the Peloponnese peninsula in the south with the rest of Greece in the north. About one-third of the country rested on the high Peloponnese area in the south and was connected to the rest of the country by the four-mile-wide isthmus at Corinth. The peninsula had several dangerous capes at its southern points. Therefore much of the trade between the eastern part of the Empire and Rome passed through Corinth rather than making the hazardous journey around the southern tip of the peninsula. Traders, travelers, sailors, stevedores, and, of course, the unemployed filled the city of Corinth.

Because of Corinth's affluence, Greek religion decided to cash in on the area. As stated in chapter three, the Greeks saw nothing wrong with sexual relationships outside marriage. They thought that no better use could be made from the profits of prostitution than to build temples.

Northeast of Corinth towered the Acropolis, and on

it, Greek religion built the great temple of Aphrodite, the goddess of "love." To this temple were attached one thousand priestesses—actually "sacred" prostitutes. Every evening they descended from the hill to the streets of Corinth to ply their trade, which brought in an excellent income for their religion. In fact, at the time of Paul's sojourn there, Corinth had become a synonym for sin, especially the sins of fast living, which include sexual immorality of all types, drunkenness, and debauchery. Here in this kind of city, Paul and his Christian friends established a church. But, as might be expected, the church in this kind of environment, though greatly needed, experienced rough going.

One of the most difficult problems was to get the people who joined the Christian church to break completely with the pagan environment which surrounded them. In the fifth chapter of first Corinthians, Paul deals with a man living with his stepmother. Of course, it is quite possible that this woman was already divorced from her husband. In any case, this man and his stepmother simply began living together. Perhaps these two expected to marry someday if they discovered they liked each other enough and were well suited in temperament so as to be harmonious. Like many people of our own day, this couple didn't see any reason to postpone sex until they were ready to commit themselves to each other in the sacred bond of marriage. Apparently they reasoned that their relationship was physically and emotionally satisfying for the moment, so what else mattered.

When the report of this relationship reached him, Paul was outraged. He told the Corinthian Christians that that kind of immorality was not even found among the pagans. (I Cor. 5:1) What he most likely meant is that there were many non-Jewish Christians who would condemn such behavior, for as we have seen, thousands of Gentiles were drawn to Judaism because of its high moral standards. Of course, on the other hand, this kind of behavior was common practice among most of the pagans, and when we add to this the practice of idolatry, we have the two basic reasons why the words "Gentile" and "pagan" were synonymous to most Jews.

To Greeks and Romans in Paul's time, as we have already noted, marriage was only an economic and legal contract between a man and woman, in which the man agreed to support the woman financially and she agreed to manage his household affairs and care for his legitimate children. The idea of sexual fidelity between them, and that they would "love and cherish each other and forsake all others," was an utterly foreign concept. That is why it was most difficult for the young church, surrounded by this vast ocean of infidelity, to keep itself "unspotted from the world."

Likewise, since each person was a divine gift created in the image of God, each was therefore precious to God and to every member of the family. But this understanding of sex as holy and divine, again, was so utterly foreign to the whole Gentile world that the young church had great difficulty preventing some of the Gentile converts from bringing their pagan lifestyles with them into the Christian faith. Yet Paul knew that for the church to survive and grow, every family in it had to be a holy family, and every convert must keep the teachings of our Lord as they had been given and exemplified by Jesus himself.

So Paul writes to the Corinthians:

> I have written you in my letter not to associate with sexually immoral people . . . not at all meaning the people of this world who are immoral, or the greedy and swindlers, or idolators. In that case you would have to leave this world. But now I am writing you that you must not associate with anyone who calls himself a brother but

is sexually immoral or greedy, an idolator or a slanderer, a
drunkard or a swindler. With such a man do not even eat.
(I Cor. 5:9-11 NIV)

In these verses, Paul is making it clear that he is
not asking the Christians to withdraw from the
pagans of the world. That would have been totally
impossible in a place like Corinth, just as it would be
in our cities and towns in the United States today. But
Paul is saying that the church must enforce Christian
standards of morality upon its own members. Christians must not allow people to come into the church
and profess faith in Jesus Christ if they intend to continue their old lifestyle.

The Corinthians must not associate with anyone
who bore the name of "brother," if he was guilty of sexual immorality, alcohol abuse, greed, slander, or thiev-
ery. When one becomes a Christian he is to put these
marks of the old pagan lifestyle out of his life. Paul
ends this paragraph with a command: "Drive out the
wicked person from among you." (I Cor. 5:13) The
church must always maintain, for everyone to see, the
starkly vivid contrast between the Christian lifestyle
and the way of life followed by non-believers.

This is one of the major problems that we face here
in the United States in the twentieth century. Our religion often has no requirements for Christians except
that they contribute to the budget and also, if conve-
nient, that they attend church worship at least part of
the time. In reality, many of us who are active leaders
in the church have given up much of the Christian
lifestyle as taught by the New Testament. At the same
time, we have adopted so much of the pagan lifestyle
from our non-Christian neighbors that the impact of
the gospel has been blunted for all of us, and totally
wiped out for many. This is true, both for the members of the church and for citizens of the community

outside the church. Therefore, we live in a time when there is often very little difference between the lifestyle of those in the church and that of the multitudes who never go near the church.

Even so, some of us pray for a time when violence will disappear from our society: we would like to live in a community where we could walk the streets of our neighborhood at night without fear of mugging or rape, and where our children could go to public school without danger of being molested or having dope constantly thrust at them. But it is time that we Christians recognize the brutal truth that all such prayers are wasted until we, and the vast majority of the followers of Jesus, are willing to adopt the Christian lifestyle so genuinely that we make the Christian way stand out in absolute contrast to the lifestyle of the pagan world about us. First century Christians made their lifestyle shine brilliantly in the blackness of pagan immorality. Until today's Christian living shows a definite contrast to pagan living, there can be no awakening to relieve our suffering. One of the problems we Christians face today is that we have so misunderstood the message of God's love that we have become completely soft on its moral standards.

God's Love Is Not Soft Love

Genuine caring love enforces laws and disciplines necessary for human welfare and survival. Sometimes we forget this basic truth and cease to be the "light of the world," becoming instead an opaque blanket preventing the world from seeing the Christ who is "The Light of the World."

Paul never lost sight of the standards of the Gospel. In this passage he speaks firmly, expressing concern that the sinning person be punished, see his error, and be "saved in the day of our Lord." Without question this kind of tough love is much closer to the genuine love of Christ than the soft, mushy kind that we sometimes have. Our love often tolerates everything and excuses everyone from following the standards of Christian living.

The early followers of our Lord were able to balance revulsion for sin with love and forgiveness for the sinner. They were determined to keep themselves untainted by Gentile lifestyles, but at the same time show the kind of caring love to the people of the world which they had found in Christ. So they insisted that new converts make a complete break with their past way of living and adopt the behavior and practices of true followers of Jesus Christ.

When the new Christian failed, his shortcomings were pointed out to him in love, and when he repented, he was forgiven and accepted back into the Christian community. Small wonder, then, that with this kind of forgiving fellowship within Christian churches, that new converts soon multiplied from thousands to hundreds of thousands.

The New Testament records letters which Paul wrote to seven of the churches which he founded. In six out of the seven, he specifically mentioned the common Gentile practice of total sexual freedom. The only letter written by Paul which does not contain any reference to this problem is the letter to the Philippians. All other young churches struggled with problems of sexual sin.

We have already mentioned what Paul said to the Romans and his exasperation with the Corinthians as reported in I Cor. 5. Now let us see what Paul said in his second letter to the Corinthians, as well as what he said to the Galatians, Ephesians, and Colossians. Here are his words:

> I am afraid that, when I come again, my God may humiliate me in your presence, that I may have tears to

shed over many of those who have sinned in the past and have not repented of their unclean lives, their fornication and sensuality. (II Cor. 12:21 NEB)

To the Galatians, Paul says:

Anyone can see the kind of behavior that belongs to the lower nature: fornication, impurity, and indecency; idolatry and sorcery; quarrels, a contentious temper, envy, fits of rage, selfish ambitions, dissensions, party intrigues, and jealousies; drinking bouts, orgies, and the like. I warn you, as I warned you before, that those who behave in such ways will never inherit the kingdom of God. (Gal. 5:19-21 NEB)

To the Ephesians, Paul writes:

Fornication and indecency of any kind, or ruthless greed, must not be so much as mentioned among you, as befits the people of God . . . For be very sure of this: no one given to fornication or indecency, or the greed which makes an idol of gain, has any share in the kingdom of Christ and of God. (Eph. 5:3, 5 NEB)

Paul writes to the Colossians:

Then put to death those parts of you which belong to the earth—fornication, indecency, lust, foul cravings, and the ruthless greed which is nothing less than idolatry. (Col. 3:5 NEB)

Nowhere in all of the writings of Paul is his statement on sexual purity more vivid than in his first letter to the Thessalonians. Today's English version puts these teachings of the great apostle in words we can understand:

Finally, our brothers, you learned from us how you should live in order to please God. This is, of course, the way you have been living. And now we beg and urge you in the name of the Lord Jesus to do even more. For you know the instructions we gave you by the authority of the Lord Jesus. God wants you to be holy and completely free from sexual immorality. Each of you men should know how to control his body in a holy and honorable way, not with lustful desire, like the heathen who does not know God. In this matter, then, no man should do wrong to his fellow Christian or take advantage of him. We have told you this before, and we strongly warned you that the Lord will punish those who do that. God did not call us to live in immorality, but in holiness. So then, whoever rejects this teaching is not rejecting man, but God, who gives you his Holy Spirit. (I Thes. 4:1-8 TEV)

In this passage, Paul states exactly what he means. He starts by relating faith and morality. Christian truth and Christian behavior must be one and the same. Paul says, "God wants you to be holy and completely free from sexual immorality." Commenting on this passage, Dr. James W. Clark says:

> The Thessalonians cannot be Christians and be sexually loose, says their great leader. Their new faith entails chastity in the unmarried, and fidelity to their vows in the married. This was revolutionary and stern teaching, for the religion from which they had been recently turned had, as its center, phallic rites . . . Immorality was not a matter for shame, rather of pride, for it was part of the ritual of temple worship.[3]

These moral demands are certainly just as applicable to us today as they were to the people of Thessalonica. What we euphemistically call "the new morality" is really the same kind of paganism Paul is describing here. Despite these clear statements there are religious leaders today who are trying to convince us that there is nothing wrong with casual sex. Some are even trying to re-program our consciences so we feel no guilt about sexual sin. Dr. James W. Clark, mentioned above, adds these words:

---

[3] Nolan B. Harmon, ed., *The Interpreters Bible* (New York: Abingdon: 1971), Vol. 11, p. 294.

> We further domesticate our conscience by covering up guilt under such fancy names as "neurosis," "psychosis," "action of the subconscious," "moral delinquency," "maladjustment," "complex," or "frustration." But despite all our callousness and evasiveness, guilt will not down . . . It exposes and condemns our generation as it did Judah.[4]

Moreover, many Christians of our time do not consider their bodies as temples of the Holy Spirit, but instead live for the thrill of the moment. Our feelings have become more important to us than anything else. Chastity is declared old-fashioned and outmoded. Freudian psychology tells us that sexual desire is a part of our nature, and that to deny its full expression, no matter with whom, is to create a sense of frustration. This may not be an entirely accurate interpretation of the teachings of Sigmund Freud, but it is the understanding that many get from hearing others talk about him.

Many teachers who do not know Christian truth say that to release our sex drive is to develop our personality. This kind of argument comes from those who do not know the history of ancient pagan civilizations. Those who follow this lifestyle have much unhappiness and also bring crime, violence, and a cheap view of human life to our entire society.

Our modern sexual freedom is creating havoc in our families. In the application of I Thes. 4:1-8, Dr. Clark emphasizes this position by saying:

> Because of widespread impurity and marital infidelity, something has happened to the American home. Its permanence and unity are being distorted, as the frequency of divorce and separation prove beyond a question. *Long-established loyalties are being surrendered, so husbands and wives are discovering they are unfit for the adventure*

---

[4] Harmon, ed., *Interpreters Bible,* p. 295.

in staunch comradeship and mutual help that marriage demands.[5] [italics added]

Other New Testament Writers Also Speak of Sexual Problems

Thus far in our study of the teaching of the early church about sex and the family, we have considered only the letters of Paul and Luke's report of the Jerusalem Conference. We must now look at other New Testament writings to see if they support the same positions as those of Paul and Luke.

An Open Letter to All Christians

The letter to the Hebrews was written to all new Christians. In this epistle one sentence serves as a guideline for all family relationships. "Marriage is honorable; let us all keep it so, and the marriage bond inviolate; for God's judgment will fall on fornicators and adulterers." (Heb. 13:4 NEB)

The author is very specific about the kinds of behavior that weaken the marriage bond. He specifically names fornication and adultery. These two practices, so common among Gentiles, were then—and still are—devastating to the marriage. Many people can learn to tolerate anger and forgive criticism coming from a spouse, but most people find it impossible to live with a mate who is persistently unfaithful. If adultery is continuous, it usually destroys the marriage.

This section of Hebrews tells us that the author is committed to keeping the family strong. To him, marriage is a sacred covenant. The marriage bond must

---

5 Harmon, ed., *Interpreters Bible,* p. 297. I have used these extensive quotes from Dr. Clark because he is one of the authors of this scholarly commentary, thought by many to be one of the most accurate biblical interpretations. I want the reader to be aware that the best biblical scholarship of today clearly identifies the "new morality" of our time with the immorality that the New Testament warns the disciples of Jesus not to follow.

be respected and family security must be given top priority. He believes that any attitude or behavior which weakens the family rests under the judgment of God. In this statement, we find the same strong conviction that monogamy is God's plan for his children that is characteristic of other New Testament writers.

Peter and Paul Agree

None of the disciples of our Lord came to have more authority or greater respect than Peter. When we find out where Peter stood in regard to any subject, we are close to the official position of the early church, or perhaps it would be better to say we are close to the consensus of the leadership of the church. Peter and Paul disagreed with each other on some things, but when it comes to teaching about sex and the family, they agree.

When Peter wrote to the Christians in Asia Minor he said, "In your past life you had ample time to follow the heathen way of life. Your conduct was characterized by shameless immorality, by giving your passions their way, by habitual drunkenness, by carousals and drinking parties, and by idolatries which outrage common decency."[6] In this passage Peter states very clearly that the Christian lifestyle must be different from the pagan lifestyle.

Peter shows real concern over what he calls "self-appointed" teachers and false teachers who are disturbing many of the new believers. He accuses these people of destructive heresies and fears that many will follow their licentiousness. He warns that false teachers are like irrational animals, creatures of instinct.

Second Peter deals with the same problem. We read: "They have eyes full of adultery, insatiable for

6 William Barclay, *The New Testament: A New Translation,* Vol. II, (London/New York: Collins Press, 1969), I Pet. 4:3.

sin. They entice unsteady souls. They have hearts trained in greed. Accursed children! Forsaking the right way they have gone astray . . ." (II Peter 2:14-15a) In this passage, the author is describing false prophets who have made their way into the young church. They are teaching false doctrines. Their minds are filled with lust and their lives with adultery. Both William Barclay and Dr. Albert Barnett, who writes the exegesis for the *Interpreter's Bible*, say that "They have eyes full of adultery" is a Greek passage, which is not translatable as far as English is concerned. What it literally says is, "They have eyes full of an adulteress." Both commentators say that the most likely meaning here is that they see in every woman a possible adulteress and are wondering how she can be persuaded to gratify their lusts.[7]

It is absolutely clear that Peter, who is one of the apostles referred to by Paul as "pillar" of the church, holds the same position on sexual sin that Paul, Luke, Matthew and other writers of the Good News. It seems clear from this passage that any church leader who would condone sex between unmarried adults would be described by Peter as a false teacher.

Small Book; Forceful Message!

Another book of the Bible which deals with the problem of sex is the little book of Jude, which was written near the end of the New Testament period. The writer, who identifies himself as a brother of James and servant of Jesus Christ, writes a general letter to "Those who are called, beloved in God the Father and kept for Jesus Christ." (Jude 1) He is concerned because certain persons have wormed their way into the church whose teaching and living are not at all

[7]Barclay, *The Letters of James and Peter,* (Westminster: 1955), p. 331; *The Interpreter's Bible*, Vol 12, (Abingdon: 1957), p. 193.

Christian. In fact, he says that they are already under condemnation and will surely receive the judgment of God.

Jude says that these persons, "pervert the grace of our God into licentiousness and deny our only Master and Lord, Jesus Christ." (verse 4b) Commenting on these persons about whom Jude is so concerned, Dr. Albert E. Barnett says:

> Their irreverence expresses itself in a perversion of *the grace of our God into licentiousness.* The Greek word here translated *licentiousness,* connotes lust and its unbridled expression in sexual intercourse. It pictures outbreaking and outrageous indecency, not merely impurity of heart.[8]

The people whom Jude is concerned about have distorted the teaching of Jesus regarding grace and forgiveness. They have completely divorced body and spirit. They are teaching that what the body does has no relation to spiritual values. They also maintain that people can be good Christians while living in lust and greed—freely indulging physical cravings—as long as they say their prayers, attend church, and take communion.

Unfortunately, this kind of error has plagued the church throughout its long history, dying out for a while and then reappearing. The persons about whom Jude is concerned did not see themselves as enemies of Christianity. They believed they were the leaders of a new spiritual elite. Jude urges all who are beloved and called of God to resist this teaching and keep the faith. In the second half of the twentieth century, the kind of persons about whom Jude was concerned have again made their way into many churches. They consider themselves deep thinkers and believe they

[8]*The Interpreter's Bible,* Vol. 12, p. 324.

are the avant-garde of a new morality. Leaders of this kind spread confusion in the minds of many (especially the young) about true Christian doctrine. They either see nothing wrong with sex between consenting adults outside of marriage, or else they have the idea that there is *no Christian doctrine* regarding the use of sex.

Nothing could possibly be farther from the truth. Jude is emphatic in contending that God has always judged and destroyed those who believed and practiced such doctrine. He is definite and clear that all such teaching and practice is under the judgment and condemnation of Almighty God. The message of Jude is just as applicable to the twentieth century as to the first century. Today we witness many evidences that loose sex is the destroyer of the family and of all human values.

The last references to sexual behavior that we have in the New Testament are found in the second chapter of the Revelation of John. In that chapter and the one following, we find letters from the Living Christ to the seven churches in Asia. (Asia was a Roman province in western Asia Minor, now part of Turkey.)

The first letter to the church at Ephesus compliments the Ephesians for hating the practices of the Nicolaitans, whose deeds Christ says he also hates. We meet this same group of people in the letter to Pergamum. However, at Pergamum some church members have actually embraced the practices of the Nicolaitans, so the enemy who is misleading Christians is now in the church, whereas with the Ephesians, the temptation was coming from outside the church.

Who were the Nicolaitans? The majority of the early fathers identify them as followers of Nicolaus, a proselyte from Cypress who was one of the seven deacons appointed to minister to the needs of widows (Acts

6:5). He became a heretic who contended that the inner life was all that was important, that the Law was superceded by Christ and no longer applied. One needed only faith in Christ; as long as he had faith, he could do anything he wished with his body. Therefore, Nicolaitans ate food offered to idols and engaged in sexual immorality (Rev. 2:14-15). Irenaeus says of the Nicolaitans, "They lived lives of unrestrained indulgence."

We meet this same problem again in the letter to the church at Thyatira.[9] Here it is couched in different metaphors. A woman who is referred to as Jezebel, a prophetess, is a leader of a group who wants to compromise with the environment in which they find themselves. She and her followers are eating meat offered to idols and indulging in sexual immorality. We must remember that these are two of the practices specifically forbidden in the letter sent by the Jerusalem Conference to all Gentile churches. (Acts 15:23-29)

We should be aware that at the time Revelation was written, at the end of the first or beginning of the second century, the matter of sexual purity was still a paramount problem for the young Christian churches. John, who was closest of all the disciples to our Lord and Savior, is speaking out very clearly on the Christian understanding of human sexuality. He is sending his message to the seven churches in the form of letters that he received from the living Christ. Clearly the disciple who knew the mind and heart of Jesus as no other person, believed that our Lord expected his followers to live lives of sexual purity.

---

[9] Barclay, *The Revelation of John,* Rev. ed. (Westminster, 1960) Vol. 1, p. 67.

CHAPTER SIX

Our Creator's Plan for Human Sexuality

In the four preceding chapters we have taken a careful look at the scriptures of both the Old and New Testaments to see what they have to teach us about human sexuality and its use in the family. We have seen that author after author, beginning with the book of Genesis and ending with the book of Revelation, has stated a definite and clear position.

We have learned that from the time when God first revealed himself to the Hebrews to the teachings of our Lord and Savior Jesus Christ, and in the writings of his disciples, there is a consistent witness about the Divine purpose of sex and its place of importance in the family. This witness is wholly consistent and never confused, either in Old Testament writings or in New Testament accounts from the apostles and disciples of our Lord.

The Bible clearly teaches that there is a specific plan for sex, which was in the mind and purpose of the Creator from the time of man's beginning, i.e. God gave us sex with definite goals for its use. Let us now consider these Divine plans and purposes as they have been presented by those leaders chosen to write the Holy Scriptures.

Creating New Persons

The first and most obvious purpose of sex according to the Divine plan is to create new life. We read:

> So God created man in his own image, in the image of
> God created he him; male and female he created them.
> And God blessed them, and God said to them, "Be fruitful
> and multiply, and fill the earth and subdue it; and have
> dominion over the fish of the seas and over the birds of
> the air and over every living thing that moves upon the
> earth." (Gen. 1:27-28)

However, with humans (unlike animals) there was an entirely new quality, since people were created in God's image. Indeed, humans are unique among all of God's creation because they alone are created in God's image. We alone are told to have dominion over all other life. We alone are capable of becoming God-like in character. We alone are capable of moving toward the kind of perfection which we see in God as revealed to us by Jesus Christ.

I find this utterly mind-boggling! The Creator of all the universe has given to us, as his children, the awesome power to enter into marriage with a person of the opposite sex whom we have chosen for the high and holy purpose of begetting new human beings, who are also then created in God's image and designed by the Creator to live forever. In these bodies, God has placed his most precious gift, the ability to create life that is not only physical and designed to live on this planet for seventy years or so, but life that is also spirit and therefore intended by our Creator to live forever.

Such is the love which God has for us, and the confidence that he has in us. When I'm discouraged or depressed, nothing inspires me more than this knowledge. My Creator loves me and made me in His image, and He gave me the power to become a creator—not just making things with my mind and hands like pianos, automobiles, or poems, but to create other persons, who according to Divine purpose will live forever.

Support for the Covenant Relationship

The second Divine purpose for sex in humans is to help provide in each home an atmosphere of love, tenderness, fidelity, and security, for sex is a powerful bonding agent between husband and wife. The Creator designed it to bring the pleasure and joy that a husband and wife can find in no other way. God did not want people to find marriage boring. But the Creator planned it to be the most rewarding, fulfilling experience which one could have in all of life. He planned for sex within marriage to bring rewards which no temporary relationship could supply, no matter how passionate the momentary thrill.

Therefore, God designed sex to give the most pleasure, joy and completeness that two people could ever experience in life. This creates a feeling of deep caring that is felt by each family member—children as well as parents. *God knew that in his universe, lasting joy, peace, and fulfillment could not be obtained from temporary relationships.* Only secure and durable relationships could bring the richest rewards that life has to offer.

In addition, persons who enter into marriage must be willing to fulfill their commitment to their mate. I believe that "to love and to cherish" refers to what one gives not what one gets. If husband and wife do not support each other in personality achievement and growth, the most exciting sexual fulfillment in the world will soon lose its luster and ultimately become repulsive. Love, care, and support must be present or sex will fade. When we fail to give spiritual support to each other, no amount of sexual thrills can fill the void.

Perhaps many fail to see the basic relatedness of sex to the whole of life, but sex plays a vital role in the creation of mature persons. It is vastly more than bodily interaction. It is really the function of the whole being of two persons who are committed to each other for the purpose of fulfilling God's dreams for both of them.

God planned sex as a holy tryst. It is not a substitute for love, humility, and good will. It is a powerful urge toward closeness and the desire to be with the loved person in tender embrace, especially through the years when the pressures of raising a family are the heaviest. For most parents, during the act of being physically one, caring increases and love grows to assist in creating total oneness of mind and spirit.

Sex is a powerful and precious bonding force when it is used in the holy tryst between husband and wife. It supports and strengthens their relationship throughout life. It is a thrilling and satisfying experience which brings pleasure, joy, peace, and unity throughout all of life, as long as fidelity lasts. But if fidelity is broken, it can easily become the most disruptive force in the relationship.

Unless we as parents are growing persons, we will not be able to cope with the problems that we face with developing children. The real test for most marriages is not in the ability of the mates to create children, but in the long, hard pull to *cope with* and *fulfill* the *physical, emotional, and spiritual needs* of the children as they grow from infancy to adult life.

During this time, parents will often disagree on how to handle the situation with which each child confronts them. So they will need constant consultation with each other at a time when the growing material needs of the family put pressure on the earning capacity of one or both parents. These growing economic demands will often rob them of much of the opportunity for being together that they had in the early days of marriage, when they just had each other and responsibilities were few. Now their obligations have become manifold and are still increasing, so they have to plan carefully for time to be with each other alone.

At this juncture of their relationship under the Divine plan, the sacred tryst of sexual communication plays a very important role in preserving their sense of unity and helps to develop growing trust and support for each other and hence the family. Because they are constantly challenged by new problems of child raising and, usually, an increasing financial burden, this is a time of real testing for every marriage—there being the added danger that by now, either one or both have drifted into the habit of taking the other for granted. The sacred and exciting tryst helps to prevent this from happening.

This is also a time when fidelity to each other is more severely tested than in the first years of marriage. In the beginning, a couple seldom doubts each other's love. Later, one or both may wonder if he or she is still loved. Moreover, there are many other persons in their age group who face the same kind of pressures. Some of these have already divorced; they are miserable in their loneliness and look for anyone who can give love, sex, and support. Some are bitter and do not care whose home they break up, as long as they can have an intimate relationship with someone again.

Thus, many homes dissolve after twelve to fifteen years of marriage, and while divorce is unpleasant for the couple who separates, it is usually a disaster for their children. For the divorced parents, there is always the hope of finding a new partner, but for the children, the most precious thing in life, their home, is gone forever. One young woman with a fine family of her own said to me, "My parents had a lot of trouble but they stuck it out for my sake until I finished high school. When I left for college, they got a divorce. I can't tell you what that did to me. I could go and visit Mom or I could go and stay with Dad, but I never had a home again. My home was gone."

Most divorcing parents, though not all, put their children through this kind of situation. Although there may be a kind and understanding stepfather or stepmother, and the children know that their real father or mother is happy with their new mate, they rarely feel the closeness of relationship which they had with their own parent. And they usually live with the fact that they have to make many decisions which will please one parent and hurt the other. I have often had to face this problem counseling the children of divorced parents; whichever way the child decides, there is pain. . . there are no winners, only losers.

As stated before, one of the major roles that our Creator assigned to sex was that of helping parents to keep a growing relationship during the stressful times of family rearing. Yet, sex is not a cure-all. It does not take the place of patience, kindness, fidelity, or prayer. It is no substitute for the humility to seek forgiveness when we have wronged the other. It does not supplant the need for compassion when we have been wronged by the other. It can never replace the vital role of humble confession: "I am wrong," or "I am sorry," or "Please forgive me."

The Bible tells us that God saw that it was not good for man to live alone, and so he provided woman as his companion. (Gen. 2:18) To them he gave the gift of sex because he knew that it was not best for them to be alone. They would grow more and reach the maturity that he had planned for them only if they entered into the task of raising a family. Therefore, sex, in the Divine plan, was and is to be both a creator and a sustainer of family life and closeness. We rejoice and give thanks to God for this glorious gift.

CHAPTER SEVEN

God's Judgment Is Inescapable

In the preceding chapter, we discussed the Divine Plan for human sexuality and learned that sex is one of God's greatest gifts. The Creator designed it to enable us to become co-creators with him in the very highest sense of personal and family development, without which there can be no society or civilization.

Further, God planned sex to be a powerful aid in bonding husband and wife in life's most supportive, rewarding, and fulfilling relationship, where each partner assists the other in personal development. In God's plan, the marriage contract, enriched by sexual union, must continue until one shall lay the other in the arms of God.

Now, we must face the terrible reality that all uses of sex except those which are in harmony with the plan of our Creator are misuses. The judgment of almighty God will come on all who prostitute sex for their own selfish pleasure without the commitment and dedication of marriage. When I speak of the judgments of God, I am using the term in a general sense as it would be applied to the violation of any of the great laws or principles of the created universe. For example, it is a law of the physical universe that as velocity (speed) doubles, braking distance quadruples. In other words, if a car's brakes will stop the car in forty feet when it is going twenty miles and hour, when the speed is increased to forty miles per hour, it will take not eighty feet, but one hundred sixty feet to stop. We have thousands of accidents and injuries and hundreds of deaths every year on our highways because drivers are either ignorant of this law or they disregard it. All such accidents are God's judgment upon those who become careless with this universal law of physics. We often call such results natural consequence. It is also important to realize that ignorance of this law or forgetting that it is always present will in no way lessen the damage when the law is violated.

In the same way, the judgment of God falls upon every person who misuses his great gift of sex, either through ignorance or willful rebellion. Ignorance or rejection of God's laws governing the use of sex will not alter the consequences or lessen the damage that comes from their misuse.

Audrey was pregnant and in her junior year in high school when she came to see me. Her home and Sunday school had taught her that sex was for marriage. However, Audrey was from a broken home. She and her stepfather did not get along well, and she longed for her real father. Her attendence at Sunday school had been very irregular.

At high school Audrey fell hard for Harold. He was an exciting boy because he told her he loved her. More than that, he was rebellious and always took her side in any disagreement she had with her parents. This made her feel close to him. She just knew she loved him and would like to marry him.

But Harold knew what he wanted. So far as he was concerned, girls were for sex, and his goal in dating was to have all the sex he wanted.

Audrey thought she was in love, but because of her training, she was afraid she would get pregnant if she went "all the way." Harold told her that a girl never got pregnant the first time she had sex. He seemed to know everything, and she believed him when he told her that it took a lot of practice before a girl had enough skill at sex to get pregnant. However, Harold's deception and Audrey's gullibility did not change the natural law that when an ovum and a sperm unite, a new life begins. It was a bitter lesson that caused suffering for Audrey and her family. She learned the hard way that the rules given in the Bible forbidding sex between singles were put there because God wants to save us from suffering and provide real security for all of his children.

As for Harold's feigned love for Audrey, once he found out she was pregnant, he refused to see her or return her frantic phone calls; Audrey learned that when Harold said, "I love you," he really meant, "I lust for your body."

Audrey's pregnancy was a terrible experience that left deep scars. I was able to help her find God's love and forgiveness, but she was still pregnant. After her baby was born and adopted by a loving, childless couple, Audrey returned to high school a wiser and more devout person who knew that God's commandments against sexual intercourse outside of marriage were given for our happiness.

The family is absolutely vital in God's creative plan for the development of every person. It is for this reason that God has given us rules by which the family should live—rules for the husband and father, rules for the wife and mother, and rules for the children. From the time of Adam and Eve's rebellion in the garden of Eden, God knew that his rules for family protection would not always be followed, so in addition to the rules, God also prepared great rewards for those who kept his rules. Those who followed God's plan had strong families, great loyalties, beautiful life-giving sacrifices, devoted love, warmth, companionship, all of which grew in value for each member of the family throughout all of life.

For those who reject God's creative love and the laws that protect family security, God also provides penalties. There is the anguish of broken relationships, the feeling of guilt and betrayal, loneliness and isolation. There are also terrible consequences for children from broken homes.

Finally, there is the possibility that if divorces increase too much and the family continues to decline, the civilization dies—which, as we have seen, it did in Greece, Canaan, and Rome. The commandments forbidding fornication and adultery are given to preserve family security. They are designed to protect growing children. They are to make possible communities where life is safe and to enable civilization to develop and endure.

God, in His great love, seeks to reach all His children and restore them to fellowship with Him. For those who are so addicted to self-seeking pleasures that they do not have any concern for these long-term consequences, that usually affect others more than themselves, God sends his judgment in more immediate and personal ways.

Apparently some of the afflictions we call venereal disease have been around for a long time. In his first letter to the Corinthians, the Apostle Paul says: "Shun fornication. Every other sin that a man can commit is outside the body; but the fornicator sins against his own body." (1 Cor. 6:18 NEB) This statement would seem to indicate that fornication caused some adverse effects in the body.

We do know that promiscuous sex in our time is spreading syphilis and gonorrhea to epidemic proportions. Moreover, medical science is hard-pressed to cope with the spread of these diseases for two reasons. First, the incubation period is long enough that by the time a person discovers he has contracted either of these diseases, those who are sexually active may have already communicated the disease to a dozen or more others, and they to others in ever-growing circles of infection. The second problem which medical science faces is that repeated exposure is steadily building immunity to the drugs used to combat the disease, so new drugs must continually be developed.

Still another problem for modern medicine, which is concurrent with the rapid rise of promiscuous sex in our time, is that we are developing new diseases, never before known, which are also sexually transmitted. In this classification we must include Herpes Simplex II (which is related to the common cold sore) and the new and deadly disease AIDS (Acquired Immune Deficiency Syndrome), which is currently reported to kill more than 75 percent of its victims within two years after it is diagnosed. This disease is so new that medical science knows very little about it and at present has no medicine with which to treat it. Even though there is a "crash program" to conquer this terrible killer, present estimates are that it may take five or more years to develop successful treatment.

These physical diseases get one's attention very quickly. They are powerful reminders that we may need to change our lifestyle. They bring the same message to those who practice promiscuous sex that delirium tremens brings to the alcoholic: "Change your ways, if you want to live."

Persons who feel free to copulate with anyone available shut themselves out of the Kingdom of God. Paul says, "Surely you know that the unjust will never come into possession of the kingdom of God. Make no mistake: no fornicator or idolater, none who are guilty either of adultery or of homosexual perversion, no thieves or grabbers or drunkards or slanderers or swindlers, will possess the kingdom of God." (I Cor. 6:9-10 NEB)

In this passage, Paul makes it clear that the unrighteous will not inherit the kingdom of God. In plain English, this means that people who reject God's plan of following the teaching and example of Jesus Christ, will not inherit the good life that our Creator has planned for all his children.

Paul becomes very specific and lists exactly what he means by "unrighteousness." He emphasizes that those who commit sexual sins (or are idolaters, thieves, greedy, drunkards, those who revile others, and robbers) will not inherit the kingdom of God. The passage also makes it clear that engaging in sexual behavior outside of marriage classifies a person as unrighteous. The Greek is very specific here. The word which the RSV translates as "immoral" and most versions of the Bible translate as "fornicators" is especially descriptive. It means a male prostitute.

Readers who are not familiar with homosexual lifestyles in our country may be surprised to know that we have male prostitutes as the Greeks did. Just as many heterosexuals will often pay for sexual service from a female prostitute, promiscuous gays often buy their sexual service from a male prostitute.

Paul emphasizes that all sexual practices outside of marriage bar those who engage in them from entering the kingdom of God. The great missionary apostle is very specific in listing fornication, adultery and homosexual practice as barriers to God's kingdom.

When I began this study of the Judeo-Christian understanding of sex, it was not my intention to discuss homosexuality. It is a very complex problem which raises heated emotions both pro and con. Many of the finest psychologists are poles apart in their explanation of its causes and ways of dealing with those who come to them for help. The Christian community is also split in liberal, evangelical, and fundamentalist churches on how to minster to gay people.

The church is also divided over whether gay behavior is approved by God or a sin against the Divine plan.

Confusion among Christians about the rightness or wrongness of homosexual practice seems rather strange to me, since I can find absolutely no uncertainty in the teachings of either the Old or New Testaments on this subject. In the Bible, homosexual behavior is always treated in the same class as fornication and adultery, as a violation of God's intention for the creative use of sex.

Homosexuality abounded in both Greece and Rome. Without doubt it is always profuse in any society which believes in sex for the thrill of the moment. Most of the Roman Emperors were homosexuals. At the time Paul was writing some of his letters, Nero was on the throne. He took a boy called Sporus, had him castrated, married him in a wedding ceremony, and took him home to his palace in royal procession. He lived with him and called him his wife. He also married a man named Pathagoras, whom he called his husband.[1] There is no doubt that homosexual behavior was as common in Corinth and Rome as it is in San Francisco or Washington, D.C. today.

Our search through past societies leads us to conclude that the percentage of homosexuals does increase rapidly when people accept the doctrine that sex is for fun without commitment. This belief which regards sex as a pleasure to be exploited between consenting adults, with no greater purpose than physical thrill, is basically in perfect harmony with homosexual practice. If the only, or even the main, purpose of sex is the satisfaction that comes from genital stimulation, then it makes little difference whether one's companion belongs to the same sex or the opposite sex. All

---

[1]For a fuller account of homosexual behavior in both Greece and Rome, see Barclay's *Letters to the Corinthians*, (Westminster: 1956) p. 60

that is needed in a partner is someone with skill in genital stimulation and, since it is impossible to produce a child through homosexual practice, there is nothing beyond the excitement of the moment for all those following this lifestyle.

Therefore, we can arrive at no other conclusion than this: The Holy Scriptures treat homosexual behavior as an aberration and include it in the same category with adultery and fornication.

Paul's letter to the Corinthians makes vivid the fantastic power of Jesus Christ. After including sexual sinners together with thieves, the greedy, idolaters, drunkards, slanderers, and robbers, all of whom shut themselves out of the Kingdom of God, he ends the passage with a shout of triumph. "And such were (past tense) some of you." From a life sullied by some or all of these sins, the Corinthian Christians had been transformed. "But you were washed, you were sanctified, you were justified in the name of the Lord Jesus Christ and in the Spirit of our God." (I Cor. 6:11) The power of Christ mediated through the loving, caring, supporting church was able to lift the worst of sinners and give them new life: the Spirit took people who exploited others, and turned them into creative, caring, supporting members of the redeeming community.

There were in Corinth and in all the New Testament churches, people who were living proof of the power of Christ to give those who trust in him the ability to begin a new life. Jesus Christ still possesses this vast creative power. He still brings new life and a second chance to those who accept and follow him.

These various categories of sinners, whom Paul says will not enter the Kingdom of God, have at least one thing in common: they are basically parasites. They live for their own immediate pleasure, and many of them do not care whom they "rip off" to gratify their sensuous desires. This is certainly true of drunkards, who will often sacrifice the precious relationships of family to the satisfaction of their immediate craving for alcohol. *Those who want sex, without commitment, often sacrifice the richest and most precious relationships in life for momentary satisfaction.* The sad fact is that this description of life in Corinth at the time of Paul is an accurate description of life in the average American city today.

I am setting forth very strong conclusions in the remainder of this chapter and also in the rest of this book. Therefore, let me try to be absolutely clear about the people whose problems I'm describing. First of all, I'm not talking about the young couple who have a date with the purpose of having a nice evening together listening to music or talking of love, but after several hours of increasing excitement, succumb to temptation and have sexual intercourse. However they clearly recognize what they have done as wrong in the sight of God; they are both sorry that it happened and try hard not to let it happen again.

Secondly, I'm not referring to the engaged couple planning for their wedding several months off who decide that they are already committed to each other and enter into the sexual relationship before the marriage ceremony. In my opinion, their marriage will be better and stronger if they are virgins at the time of the wedding. However, I do not believe that those who enter the sexual relationship before their wedding, but only with the one to whom they are committed, will necessarily find fidelity difficult after marriage.

On the other hand, a new study of life in Sweden, where cohabitation before marriage has been in vogue longer than in the United States, indicates that couples who cohabit before marriage have problems with commitment:

A National Bureau of Economic Research study found that couples who live together before marrying have nearly 80 percent higher divorce rate than those who do not.

Information for the study was gathered in Sweden, where cohabitation reportedly is more common than in the United States. But the authors point out that the trend is similar in this country, where cohabiting has quadrupled in the past decade.

"We are not saying in any way that cohabiting causes higher divorce rates," said a Yale sociologist who is one of the study's authors. He added, "What we are saying is that it appears that people who cohabit premaritally are less committed to the institution and are more inclined to divorce than people who do not live together."[2]

In essence, then, the conclusions in this chapter and the rest of this book apply only to those who accept complete sexual freedom from the teen years until marriage as a normal and acceptable way of life.

It is my firm conviction that all persons who use sex for the pleasure of the moment, without commitment to the Divine purpose, destroy their own ability to commit themselves to another person in life-long dedication, i.e., most people who use sex early in life with any willing person become incapable of life-long intimacy with one mate. They repeatedly have to find new partners who can give them greater thrills. A lifetime of marriage counseling convinces me that this lifestyle is more addicting than marijuana, alcohol, or even heroin. Most of those who get married and resolve to be true to their mate find that their resolve "not to cheat" lasts about as long as the proverbial New Year's resolution. As with most other enslavements, only the power of God and the support of a loving, caring community can enable one to escape the deadly grip of promiscuous sex and live as a new per-

---

2 "New Findings Support Old Teachings," *The United Methodist Reporter,* Vol. 134, No. 29, Dec. 18, 1987, p. 2. Used by permission.

son in a monogamous lifestyle.

Breaking the habit of sex with other consenting persons to become a faithful mate involves re-education of the mind, rebirth of the spirit, and hardest of all, a total 180 degree change in behavior and lifestyle. This change is so difficult that, if there remains anywhere in the consciousness or thinking of the person even a shadow of a doubt about whether the past behavior was really wrong, then so long as that is true, he will be condemned to failure in his efforts to achieve fidelity in marriage.

These two lifestyles are so radically opposite that they can never co-exist in the same person. One or the other will sooner or later conquer and hold first place.

What the past experience of the human race teaches and what the Bible makes very clear is what we are now learning from the statistics on divorce developing in our own country. Those who adopt the sexual lifestyle of the Canaanites, Greeks, and Romans in the naive belief that they are following a "new morality" and have been emancipated by the pill from old requirements, are simply destroying their capability of ever being loyal and faithful mates.

Followers of the "new morality" accept the belief that the only thing wrong with sex for fun, with another willing adult, is having an unwanted child. This unwanted event can now be prevented with birth control pills or, if the pill fails, the situation can be legally relieved by abortion. Therefore we can have all the sex we want with no damage done.

Many men and women who accept the "new freedom" believe that sex is given so we can find pleasure whenever we can find a partner with similar interests. They think that marriage is only for the purpose of child-raising. Such persons like to play with sex for a number of years with many companions. Finally, they find someone whom they enjoy in other ways. Then they eventually decide that they would like to have a family, so they stop the pill and if pregnancy follows, they decide to get married and promise to "love and cherish each other and keep themselves only for the other as long as both shall live."

These sacred vows are usually kept for a while—a few months or sometimes for a few years. But most of those who come to marriage via this route discover that they have been so emasculated of fidelity by their former lifestyle that they are no longer capable of lasting loyalty and devotion.

In a few months or years, after a quarrel or two, one or the other reverts to their former mode of life. Long before the children can get through puberty, they divorce and go their separate ways. One or both have been so spiritually "neutered" by the "new morality" that they are incapable of the commitment and fidelity that marriage requires.

In the early part of this century when male chauvinism was more dominant than today, many men played the field sexually before marriage. However, when those who followed this pattern finally decided that they wanted to settle down and have a family, they always tried to find a virgin woman to marry. These were days when there was clearly a double standard. These men knew by instinct that a woman who had slept with other men could not be trusted to be a faithful wife. Her interest might easily wander to some other man. What they did not seem to realize was that their own capability of fidelity had also been mortally wounded.

We now know that there is no double standard where addiction to sex is concerned. A large percentage of both males and females who have played the field before marriage find themselves incapable of fidelity after marriage. The forty percent divorce rate in our country today confirms this fact. Those who do not know history are condemned to re-live it. Neither their own willpower nor the repeating of marriage vows is sufficient to make the radical change in lifestyle necessary for them to escape the path they have been following through the most formative years of their lives.

Since this disaster overtakes so many people and destroys their marriages, every person needs to decide by the time he or she reaches puberty whether he or she wants to be a playboy or playgirl, or whether they want to be parents and raise children in a loving, caring home where there is concern and respect for every member of the family. Anyone can have either, but no one can have both without a total transformation of their character, lifestyle, and, usually, a change of friends. *Strong, loving, caring families have seldom been created by people who believe that sex for a night of pleasure is all right for consenting adults.* This is the way it was in Jesus' time, and this is the way it is today.

Still, most of us need to actually see how the "new morality" affects our families today. In the next chapter we will look at three couples whose lives were turned inside out by one or the other mate's lifestyle of sexual freedom before marriage. Names, places, and other means of identification have been changed to protect the privacy of each person.

CHAPTER EIGHT

Divine Principles At Work Today

The distant ringing of the telephone grew louder and louder, until I awoke enough to reach to the night stand beside my bed. It was 1:30 a.m. I recognized the deeply troubled voice of John. "Jane and I are in trouble again," he said. Without stopping, he poured out the horrible events leading up to this moment.

"When I returned home from work, Jane was missing. After I made a late supper and fed our three hungry children, I obtained a babysitter and started hunting for Jane. More than three hours later I finally found her in a bar in the company of another man, and both of them were well intoxicated."

At John's insistence that they needed immediate help, I dressed and went to their home. What a terrible night for both of them! John was angry and hurt. Jane was sullen, defiant, and drinking tomato juice to sober up enough to talk coherently. She insisted that she had no future with John. She wanted out. John provided well for his family. Although not as warm and affectionate as some men, kindness flowed from his heart. He sincerely tried to be the best husband and father that he knew how to be. Tonight his anger burned hot because he felt betrayed. However, he was not violent or abusive. Because of his Christian upbringing, he believed that marriage was for keeps. He knew he needed to make changes, and he wanted them both to seek counseling.

All of John's efforts made little impression on Jane. During the previous two years, she had committed adultery with anybody who was willing. She said that she knew it was a sin, for she had been raised in the Catholic Church and her upbringing had been rather strict. She definitely knew right from wrong, but she was powerless to do right and reject wrong.

Most of Jane's high school friends had been sexually active. Her mother had always taught her never to bring an unwanted baby into the world; that was the thing that really registered in Jane's sixteen-year-old mind—preventing unwanted pregnancy, not the immorality of sexual promiscuity.

By this time the birth control pill was on the market. Several of Jane's mid-to-late-teen girlfriends had obtained them. They were telling her how exciting sex was and urging her to join them in this kind of fun. We do not know for sure whether Jane became sexually active at this time. But we do know that a seed had been planted in her mind. She now believed that sex outside of marriage was OK as long as one did not get pregnant. Apparently she never lost this idea, even after she and John were married. Even though she had told me that she knew adultery was a sin, her resolve to be faithful in marriage had been so weakened that she was unable to live by her earlier faith.

Just after Jane finished high school she met John. For the first time in her life she found a man who was really interested in her as a person. He treated her like a lady, and she found this most satisfying, so she kept seeing John and their friendship grew. Soon they realized that something wonderful and deep had developed between them. Jane began attending John's Protestant church and enjoyed the friendly people there. After a short courtship, she and John married in his church and continued faithful attendence.

In about eleven months, their first child was born.

The baby girl kept Jane busy, and she learned much about life. She and John were getting along quite well and both adored their daughter. Two years later a second daughter came into their lives. With her coming, life became more complicated for both of them. Jane now found her time almost totally involved with her two girls.

John's work at his company was increasing, as was his paycheck. He usually came home tired, just wanting to rest and enjoy his family. Before long a healthy boy arrived to bless their family. Jane was thrilled, for she especially wanted a son. However, with the added load of responsibility, Jane found it harder and harder to cope with three young children who could do very little for themselves and demanded all of her time and energy. Although John tried to help her with the children, she became more irritable. She had never before realized the enormous responsibility involved in having a family.

About this time, Jane started missing the carefree life she had found so exciting in the years before she met John. Instead of being overjoyed that all John wanted to do was to come home and spend the evening with her and the children, she gradually became bored with family living. She wanted to go out to nightclubs and dances, but John always seemed to be too tired. This led to quarrels. John wanted to find their social life in church groups, but Jane found their Christian friends too tame for her. As their arguments and disagreements increased, their sex life decreased. John still felt they had an adequate marriage, but Jane became more and more morose.

One day when John was at work, Jane had a visit from a neighbor who worked nights. He was a friendly type and after a couple of beers, he came right to the point. He wanted sex and thought she might be interested too.

Spurred on by an argument she and John had had the night before, Jane fell prey to this temptation. All she could think of saying was, "Come back right after lunch when the children are taking their naps." From then on, Jane and the neighbor had regular dates until they were caught by their spouses.

The night I arrived at their home at 2:00 a.m., Jane knew she was through with John. Other men were too much fun. She soon got her divorce.

What Jane didn't know, she learned a couple of years later. She had little trouble finding another man who would marry her, and as soon as her final divorce decree was in her hands, she married a man who was highly sociable and liked her kind of parties. But Jane found it impossible to live with him for very long. Soon she was with man number three, and this time she couldn't be bothered with the formalities of marriage. They just started living together. Jane now discovered that she was incapable of living with any man for more than a year or so. As a matter of fact, most of her "live-ins" lasted less than a year.

In all of this, the children suffered intensely. They never knew what sort of man Mom would want them to call "father." They couldn't change their love and loyalty from one father-figure to another as fast as their mom could change lovers. But then, their Mom never had real love or loyalty, all she had was sex. One by one the children moved back home to live with their father. But the scars they have from their mother being unable to fulfill a marriage commitment are still with them. The oldest is now past thirty years of age and the youngest is in his mid-twenties, but none of them has ever wanted to get married and make a home. For them, home was a painful place.

John eventually married a lovely woman. He found someone with the high ideals regarding love, home, religion, and marriage that matched his. Together they have grown in their commitment to God and to each other. They have been married nearly twenty-one years now, and their love and life grows more precious with each passing year.

Sally and George came into my life when I was in a high school/college youth group in a small church, so I knew them well, and we kept in touch through many years. Sally grew up in a Christian family in a midwestern town, so small she might be considered a farm girl. She and all her family faithfully attended both church and Sunday school. In fact she and her brothers and sisters were at church almost every time the door opened. She was a good student at high school, and being an outgoing, vivacious young lady, she had more than her share of boyfriends. Her dates were usually friends of the family or boys she met at church. However, in her early twenties, she and her family moved to another state where she found work in a large city.

All of her life, Sally had dreamed of some day meeting the right man and getting married. She wanted to be a mother and homemaker more than anything else in the world. Other women could be career people if they chose, but for her, a home and family where she could give her love to a devoted husband and growing children was all she ever wanted in life. She often wondered if she would know the right person when he came along. Meanwhile, she prepared herself for that longed-for family by the things she did at home. She became an excellent cook and a better-than-average housekeeper.

One morning a handsome young man became an employee of the company where Sally worked. George immediately noticed her and didn't waste any time asking her for a date. Many more dates followed. George found Sally especially interesting because she was different from any girl he had ever gone with. He had had many girlfriends, each of whom held his interest for a few days to a few weeks, and then one or the other of them found someone else they liked better. Sally not only had physical beauty, she also had a radiance that came from deep within. George was fascinated and intrigued. He had never before been attracted to a girl who had absolute moral standards. With his other girlfriends, sex was the order of the night, after the first date or two. But Sally had standards and stayed with them. This only increased George's determination to learn more about this lovely person. He visited her home often and began going to church with her and her family. For the first time in his life he became interested in religion and, after a few months, decided that he wanted to become a follower of Jesus Christ.

George's enthusiastic sincerity brought many changes in his life. He talked with Sally's minister, who led him into a Christian commitment. He was baptized and joined the church. A short time later they had a lovely church wedding.

Within a few months, George decided to stop smoking. This was a battle because he had become a chain-smoker in his early years in high school. But Sally helped him and he finally won the war with nicotine.

Sally and George wanted children and soon Sally became pregnant, but about the third month she had a miscarriage. This was a terrible disappointment to her, but she reasoned that others had survived the same thing, and so would she. Several months later she was again pregnant, and again had a miscarriage. Finally, Sally went to a doctor who discovered that she had syphilis, which George had acquired from one of his earlier girlfriends and thus infected her.

They both began taking treatments, but in the 1930s the treatment for syphilis was slow. It was months before they were both rid of the disease. After their ordeal of treatments ended and their doctor finally pronounced them healed, Sally wanted to have a baby. Although they tried for years, she never became pregnant again. Apparently her reproductive system had sustained irreversible damage from the disease George had brought her. With their goal of having a family thwarted, a new idea of service to others began forming in their minds and hearts. Since Sally had only completed high school and George had dropped out after his sophomore year, they attended night school. After years of struggle, George earned his BA. degree and Sally received her Associate of Arts while working full time to help support them.

Immediately after George's graduation, the mission board of their church assigned them to a settlement house ministry in the poor section of a large Asian city. There followed difficult years of learning the language, and the work with the poverty stricken taxed their strength to the utmost. While Sally was inwardly prepared for the constant drain, George had been more caught up in the glory of helping others than in the time-consuming, spirit-draining task of serving the needs of the disinherited. He found the burden almost unbearable, so when an opportunity came for employment in an exciting job at a local radio station, he took it and left the settlement house and his work with the mission board of his church.

George, a highly intelligent, friendly, outgoing person, soon made friends in his new job. He began meeting many people who had the same kind of lifestyle as the one he had known before he met Sally. Soon he had to travel to other cities and be gone for several days at a time. At first he took Sally with him. Later, however, he had to be gone at times when she could not accompany him.

Finally one day, when George was away, Sally

received a letter from him which shattered her world. George confessed that he had met a girl he loved very much; therefore, he wanted out of their marriage. He told her it would be best for her to return to her parents back in the states. Sally was devastated, but she knew that the great love she and George had shared for fifteen years was real. She was sure George would eventually return to her, so she managed to get a job to support herself and struggled on, waiting, praying, and hoping for a reunion. After all, they had shared so much and had gone through difficult times together. Years went by and Sally continued working alone and hoping that some day George would return to the wonderful life they had shared. After more than a decade, George finally sent divorce papers, which he had obtained in still a different foreign country.

This made it clear to Sally that George had returned to his old lifestyle—the one he had lived by until he'd met her. The addicting power of sex had again captured George and imprisoned him for the rest of his life.

His situation was much like that of the man of whom Jesus spoke when he said:

> When the unclean spirit has gone out of a man, he passes through waterless places seeking rest; finding none he says, "I will return to my house from which I came." And when he comes he finds it swept and put in order. then he goes and brings seven other spirits more evil than himself, and they enter and dwell there; and the last state of that man becomes worse than the first. (Luke 11:24-26 RSV)

So George wandered on through life, a lonely man who finally arrived at old age when the urges of the body decline and slowly die. He had lots of sex while it lasted, but in later years he had no home and no one who cared for him. He never knew the joy of children or the thrill of loving grandchildren climbing on his knee. For him sex had come and finally gone, leaving him empty and alone.

Because we knew George well and loved him, the loneliness and isolation which were his only companions in the latter years of his life brought us much sorrow. His tragic experience gave us a deeper appreciation of God's plan for sex. How beautiful and wonderful God's way is when we follow it in all of life's experiences. Year after year it grows in its power and ability to bless and enrich our lives. It blesses us with joy and happiness which words cannot describe: companionship, loving children, adoring grandchildren, and eternal life.

Another marriage typical of many today is that of Tom and Mary. Tom grew up in a small town in an affluent middle-class family. His parents were active in church and community life. Tom attended church and was popular in public school. His home towered above many in happiness and togetherness, as his father and mother helped each other in the family business. Tom did not have any visible conflict with his parents, and from first grade through high school, he got better than average grades and was a good athlete. In both family life and in community relationships, we would have to rate Tom's growing up experiences as being among the best and most wholesome that an American family can provide.

Mary's home also represented the typical middle-class American family. Her father, a professional worker, made enough money for the family without her mother having to leave home to supplement the income. Hers was a devoutly religious family. Both parents were active in church and community affairs. Mary was an average student and had many friendships with her peers, whom she met easily. She spent all her elementary school years in one community, and then, when her father took a job in another medium-sized town, she made new friends in high school.

When Mary graduated from high school as an average student with a far above-average mind, she went to a church-related college where she met Tom. His popularity on campus brought a real thrill when he asked her for a date. Their courtship lasted for about a year and a half, culminating in a large church wedding. Numerous presents and abounding joy seemed to give their marriage a good start. Tom, like his parents, had a better than average income. So, as a baby son and two daughters arrived in the first six years of married life, Mary was able to devote all her time to Tom and the children.

However, problems began to develop within the marriage soon after their first child arrived. As a senior in high school and through his college days, Tom became interested in the sexual revolution. From the magazines he read and the friends he associated with, he came to the conclusion that the teachings of his church about sex being for marriage only were passe and belonged to the extremes of a Victorian past. The "Pill" was available, and young people enjoyed sexual freedom with anyone who "turned them on" without any fear of being embarrassed by pregnancy. Rather than feeling guilty, his numerous experiences with various young beauties gave him a feeling of exhilaration and the assurance that he was really a man.

When he fell in love with Mary, Tom made a clear resolve that his days of playing the field were over and now he would be true to his beloved and become a good family man and an ideal father. He was sure that this was the ultimate in life and that his previous sexual experience had prepared him to be a better lover for his wife. However, shortly after their son arrived, Tom began cheating. Not often, just once in a while.

But soon he was lying about his late nights at the office, and he eventually got caught. Mary was doubly hurt—wounded by the infidelity and devastated by the lies.

Their relationship had sustained a mortal wound. Yet, Tom promised that it would never happen again. Mary believed in marriage for life, and so, after much thought and prayer, she decided to give Tom another chance.

Things were better for a while, and they decided that maybe another child would draw them closer. However, soon after their first lovely daughter was born, Tom simply couldn't resist his urges and again began his double life. He would be more careful this time, he vowed, and Mary would never know. But of course, not much time passed until he was caught again. By now the marriage was in real jeopardy because Mary found it much harder to forgive Tom, and almost impossible to trust him.

For a period of about six months, Tom was a faithful husband while he and Mary worked hard to rebuild their relationship. They moved to a new home, bigger and nicer than their old one. Both became more active in their church, and they added another lovely daughter to their family. For a year or two the rapport between Tom and Mary greatly improved. Mary had hope that, at last, they could make it and have a good marriage after all.

In the end, however, Tom's addiction to sex proved too powerful to resist, and he returned to his old behavior. Finally, after counseling and the years of trying, Mary came to the end of all feeling for Tom. He had finally succeeded in killing the great love she had had for him and utterly destroying her trust in his word. All belief and hope that he would ever be able to reform and be faithful to her died. There was simply no use in trying any longer. She sued him for divorce and was awarded custody of their three children.

Life was now greatly changed for the children, who moved with their mother to a new town. Although Tom paid a fixed amount of child support, Mary went to work to provide for herself and the children. The children visited their father on specified weekends and spent a month or two of their school vacation with him. But again and again the children were confronted with having to decide which parent they would hurt. If they decided one way, Mother would be hurt. If they chose the other alternative, Dad would be hurt. So, although they always had a house to live in, they never knew peace and harmony in family life.

The devastation caused by divorce compels one to do a lot of serious thinking. The loss of Tom's family was an earth-shaking blow to him, as he had always pictured himself as the head of a very prosperous and loving family—a good father and real leader in his community. He now believed that his problem was that he had really been unfortunate in the choice of a wife, and that if he could just find one who was more liberal and understanding, he could still become the head of one of the leading families in the community.

He looked for a woman who might understand his sexual needs and his feelings as a member of the "liberated generation." He soon found a young woman who had a good job and seemed to be at home in the business world. Susan was ten years younger than Tom, and after a short courtship, they were married and had several happy years together. Having given up her career, Susan wanted children, and soon a daughter was born.

However, Tom proved true an old biblical proverb: "The sow, after a wash, rolls in the mud again." (II Peter 2:22 NEB) Tom just could not resist sex with any beautiful and willing woman he met. He simply couldn't be true to Susan, and she could no more understand why he preferred other women to her than Mary could. Tom couldn't understand Susan either. He had provided for her a nicer home than she had ever had and more affluence than she had been accustomed to when she was working, so what more could a woman want?

Susan, on the other hand, could not see why Tom couldn't give her the one thing she really wanted—a mate who was loving and understanding, who would be faithful to her. After suffering several years of pain and humiliation, when Tom's promises to be faithful were always broken, Susan got a divorce. Once again a child was confronted with the fact that, while she loved both her parents, they did not love each other, and she would never again have a home with two, loving parents.

For a number of years Tom has been living alone, although he is not happy. He does seem to have accepted the fact that his addiction to sex outside of marriage will not be tolerated by any woman who agrees to be his wife. He now knows that he is incapable of being a faithful husband. And besides, he can get the only part of sex that he is capable of enjoying almost any night for no more than the price of a nice dinner.

However, there is a sadness in his life, for although he came from a loving and stable home, and he knows other people in his own generation who have loving and secure relationships, he himself is incapable of this kind of life. He has been a playboy too long to change. His sexual lifestyle makes his dream of a life-long, loving companionship in the beauty of a holy marriage a total impossibility. Without that radical change, which only genuine repentance and total commitment to the living Christ can produce, in the human heart, mind, and spirit, he is and will remain totally disqualified from ever being able to have an enduring, mutually precious, and growing relationship with any woman, no matter how excellent her qualifications in personal, emotional, and mental maturity.

What Tom and Mary, John and Jane, and Sally and George have learned is identical with the discoveries of millions of others: the addicting power of sex for pleasure without commitment rests under the judgment of Almighty God and brings nothing but destruction. The commandments we find in the Bible, which forbid all sexual behavior which isn't within the divinely blessed, sacred commitment of marriage, are put there by a gracious and loving Creator who wants the highest fulfillment for all of his children. God does not deny us any wholesome pleasure. He wants all his children to have lives filled with joy, peace, and happiness.

The only kinds of behavior in which God forbids us to engage are those which bring harm either to us or others.

Hence, God's Holy Word tells us not to do violence to our neighbor. We may not steal his property, bear false witness against him, commit adultery with his wife, or covet his possessions. Jesus expressed the old law in a greatly simplified and very positive form when he said that we should do unto others what we want them to do unto us. He also said that all of the commandments could be reduced to just two: to have a supreme reverence and love for God, our Creator; and to love and revere our neighbor and care for his well-being as earnestly and sincerely as we love and care for our own.

Throughout the early church as new Christians tried to apply and interpret the teachings of Jesus, it was recognized that all behavior which supported the growth and development of body, mind, and spirit was approved for Christians. But the sexual sin of copulation between singles was strictly forbidden, both to Jews and Gentiles. It was forbidden because it destroys a person's capability of being faithful to a mate in a monogamous family. It is forbidden because of the particular way it damages a person's ability to participate in a life-long commitment with a mate for the purpose of raising children in a home where there is enduring love and care for every member.

The judgments of God rest on *all* who break this law, not because he wants to rob us of pleasure, but because he wants to ensure our true happiness and that of every member of our family, and at the same time make possible the development of human civilization. We need to remember that no judgment of God is ever retributive. All his judgments are redemptive; they are designed to get our attention, bring us to our senses, and lead us back to our Father's house. What else should we expect from the God who loves us so much that he sent his beloved and sinless Son, Jesus, to die on the cross to break our enslavement to sin.

But someone will say, "I know wonderful people—some of whom are totally promiscuous and others who are homosexuals—who are kind and generous and thoughtful of others." I agree. I know people like this, too. I also know some wonderful, loving, loyal, and big-hearted people among the dozens of alcoholics with whom I have counseled throughout my life as a pastor, but for them, liquor had become their master instead of their servant, and we cannot serve two masters.

God tried to reach them through the misery of their suffering to get them to change their lifestyles and become masters of the cravings. I'm glad to say that God was able to reach many and give them freedom to become the persons he created them to be, although others rebelled—until death claimed them. But God did not want them to follow that course. Why should we be surprised when sickness or disease befalls us when we misuse our God-given gift of sex—whether that misuse is heterosexual or homosexual.

Above all of the suffering and disease, we should hear God's loving call, "My son, my daughter, I love you, come home." And through the sufferings of broken homes, sick bodies, and even dying civilizations, many hear God's voice and return to the Father's house where there is music, feasting, and dancing. However, not all of those enslaved to alcohol, sex, or some other tyrant come to their senses and return home. Many die in the far country.

But this is not the Father's will. He is always waiting for us to choose to return to the life he has prepared for us. Most often we discover that the pleasures which the Father forbade, but which we are sure will bring happiness and freedom, have ended up enslaving us—robbing us of that which we most longed for.

In the first chapter of Romans, Paul says, "For the wrath of God is revealed from heaven against all ungodliness and wickedness of men who by their wickedness suppress the truth." (Rom. 1:18) As we read the rest of the chapter, we discover that Paul is especially concerned with sex outside the marriage commitment and with envy, malice, murder, strife, and other types of behavior that hurt people. We must conclude once more that all use of sex which is not in accordance with the Creator's plan for the continuation and development of humans in loving, nurturing families, rests under the judgment of God and will bring nothing but suffering and disappointment upon all who indulge in it.

I see no reason for us to be surprised that God would visit his judgment on all who misuse his glorious gift of sex. God does not tolerate the misuse of any of his wonderful gifts. For example, the human mind is one of God's richest gifts. Through this gift, God lifted every homosapien out of the animal realm and made him a person, able to create and build great civilizations. But what a curse the mind turns out to be when it is focused on self-serving ends with no concern for others. Then man becomes lower than the beast, and he will rape, murder, kidnap, or defraud his neighbor. Auschwitz, Buchenwald, and other torture chambers bear mute testimony to the utter depravity and cruelty of the human mind when it is prostituted to goals other than those our Creator planned for it. Yet, the human mind can produce great art, inspiring music, healing medicine, and all of the thousands of other things which man has made, through which he enriches both his neighbors and himself.

Similarly, a healthy appetite is a gift from God to help us grow from babies to adults and to keep us healthy and strong. But misused, an appetite can become a curse. Recently, our television news gave the account of a man who liked to eat so much that he reached a world record weight of 1025 pounds. He was bedfast, and others had to wait on him because after he passed 800 pounds, his legs and feet could no longer bear his great weight. So, for the craving of the moment he misused God's gift of a healthy appetite.

One Sunday evening many years ago, my wife, Anna, went to a small church in our community. She heard the young minister give a quotation, without any source, which neither of us has ever forgotten. He said, "Knowledge is a divinity stolen from the altar of the gods which brings a curse on all who possess it without love." A good example of this is our knowledge of the atom and how to split it and fuse it. Our whole world shudders with fear under the shadow of the mushroom cloud, because we fear it will be used without love—perhaps even by accident or misjudgment.

Likewise, human sexuality is not stolen. It is the gift of a loving, beneficent Creator, but when used without the caring love of commitment and marriage, it brings a curse of brokenness, loneliness, suffering, and often violence on all who so use it.

How My Thinking Has Changed

When I began the research on this book, I had several goals in mind. I was aware of a lot of confusion about sexual behavior which had resulted in suffering for several members of my own family. I also felt concern for many others who came to me with broken lives and relationships. Because of the pain experienced by people very dear to me, I wanted to help by sharing the teachings of the Christian faith.

A second prod, which propelled me to engage in weeks and months of research, grew out of an experience I had as an eight-month interim pastor in a church I had previously served for fifteen years. While in this temporary ministry, I became aware that there had been a significant change in the attitudes of many church people toward sexual behavior in the five years since I had retired.

During my active ministry, Christian people accepted Biblical teaching about sex and the family. Transgressions of these rules often occurred, but they were clearly recognized as deviant behavior. People in trouble would come to confess their sins and seek God's forgiveness and restoration to his love.

Now, five years later, many people raised in Christian families were in confusion. Some were trying to live by the "new morality" in a new day of "sexual freedom." They did not think of sexual relations with a

friend as sinful or wrong. They believed they were following new truth that current society had just discovered. They were living in a new age of enlightenment.
In short, they had convinced themselves that a new
light had dawned and they were walking in its rays.
The thing that bothered them was not a sense of sin,
but the pain of broken relationships. They and their
families were in turmoil. People were angry at each
other, and confused because they could not understand why all their loved ones could not accept their
new lifestyle.

I began to search through the Bible because I knew
there were many passages dealing with the kinds of
problems people are facing today, although I had
never made a detailed study of what the scriptures
had to say about human sexuality. I now wanted to
look at all the passages dealing with sexual behavior
as it related to family stability and to God's laws for
human happiness. I knew that in God's word I would
find guidelines that would prove helpful to many who
looked to their faith for answers to their problems.

A Surprising Discovery

What I have discovered is that in the Bible we do
not find religious answers to the problems involved in
sexual behavior. What we do discover is truth about
human sexuality and family solidarity. Jesus said,
"You shall know the truth, and the truth will make
you free." (John 8:32) Truth is universal—timeless. It
does not apply only to people who want to be religious.
It applies to all people in all situations at all times. It
is equally applicable to believers and non-believers.

For example, the law of gravity is truth. Sir Isaac
Newton, the English philosopher and mathematician
of the 17th century, formulated this law as follows:
"All masses of matter attract all other masses of matter with a force which varies directly as the product of

their masses and inversely as the square of the distance between them." This law, like all truth, is universal. It arrived in the dawn of creation as part of God's plan for an orderly cosmos. It is a fact of the material universe. Long before Sir Isaac Newton, if Adam let an apple slip from his hand, it fell to the ground.

So far as the truth of gravity is concerned, it not only affects all matter but also all people and every living thing. Since the law is universal, it does not matter whether its author Sir Isaac was a Protestant, Catholic, Jew, Mohammedan, or an atheist. If I miss my step, I'll fall, no matter whether I'm religious or irreligious—and whether I know anything about Sir Isaac Newton's law or not.

This study has driven me to the conclusion that the great principles of the Bible guiding sexual behavior are also universal truths. What Old Testament writers proclaimed, what Jesus and his disciples clearly taught about human sexual behavior, is universal. "Shun fornication; do not commit adultery" apply to all people whether religious or agnostic. Moreover, these laws have the same bearing on people of our time that they had on people of ancient times. These principles will affect all people as long as life exists, for without them, family life disintegrates. Where family life collapses, civilization dies.

Wherever people, without commitment to marriage, have used sex for the physical thrill of orgasm with anyone willing to join them in pursuit of temporary excitement, family life dies, relationships are torn apart, children lose their security, and civilization collapses. This was true among Canaanites. It destroyed the Greek family. It poisoned the families of Rome and precipitated the crash of Roman civilization. In our country it is a major factor in raising our divorce rate from less than ten to forty percent in sixty-five years.

In essence, this ancient Gentile philosophy of sex for the fun of the moment has permeated our society and the thinking of many people, and it is creating the same results in our society that it produced in earlier civilizations. We now have millions of broken homes with nearly half of our children being raised by one parent or one parent and a step-parent. These children are denied the secure loving family which is every child's birthright. Even worse, we now have millions of sexually abused children. According to a recent TV news report, one girl out of every three, and one boy out of every four, in our country today will be sexually abused before the age of eighteen. Most of these children are molested by older members of their family. Statistics show that the very people children should be able to love and trust are their chief abusers.

We are now in the process of teaching young children how to protect themselves from their own parents, step-parents, uncles, aunts, brothers, and sisters. The ancient belief that sex is for physical thrills, now accepted by a large segment of our population, is the primary cause of the alarming rise in sexual abuse of children. If sex is really for pleasure with anyone you like, then why not with children.

There is absolutely nothing in the doctrine of sexual freedom to protect any child. Porn magazines teach that what we call "sexual abuse" is ideal behavior. Many of our people, both adults and children, are reading these publications, and experimenting with their teachings.

A child's only protection is found in accepting and obeying the great principles of sexual behavior given in God's Holy Word. In families where these precepts are followed, there is no child abuse. In homes where these principles are not followed, children can expect to be exploited for the pleasure of others.

Another problem we face, which is typical of all cultures which practice sexual freedom with any willing person, is the enormous rise in crimes of violence against persons. This should not surprise us. Persons who reject the belief that sex is a holy, beautiful gift of our Creator will accept sex as mere instinct to be exploited for physical gratification. Those who have this understanding of sex cannot possibly be expected to believe that the life created by sex is holy and to be respected.

If I do not respect God's gift of sex as holy, how can I possibly think that the lives produced by sex are holy and precious? Those who exploit sex for personal gratification will also use people for selfish pleasure. The value of persons as sons and daughters of God can exist only where God is adored and his principles respected.

Both men and women who adopt a promiscuous lifestyle from their mid-teen years to the time of their marriage find themselves unable to completely leave this lifestyle after marriage. They have become so accustomed to running from the tough problems of a relationship like selfishness, anger, jealousy, disappointment, and the need to forgive and ask for forgiveness, that they cannot face the difficult problems involved in marriage. During the most formative years of learning how to relate to the opposite sex, they have lived by a "use and discard" lifestyle. So they marry and divorce, and then remarry and divorce again. Finally they reach the conclusion that it is too expensive to go through the legal process so often, so many of them go through the rest of life with a series of live-ins.

This research has convinced me, and I hope it will convince you, that the Biblical commandments: "thou shalt not commit adultery" and "abstain from fornication" are universal principles for the life and protection of the family. It does not matter whether a person is religious or irreligious, when these principles are violated family life is destroyed, children and women are exploited, men are de-humanized. Finally, civilization perishes.

CHAPTER TEN

Breaking the Power of the Past

There is no question that, for many people, this book has thus far painted a gloomy picture. I am convinced that addiction to sex for fun, without commitment, is one of the most absolute forms of bondage we know, and my observation that few of us can break its grip by our own strength or willpower is true.

Some of you are saying, "I have been promiscuous. I have experienced bad relationships. When strong differences arise between me and a companion, I feel the urge to run. However, I'm tired of the recurring periods of loneliness and despair caused by my temporary relationships. Do I have any hope of becoming able to have a lasting relationship?"

We Christians have to answer that question with a triumphant and joyous "yes." This is the fantastically good news that we have in Jesus Christ. From the very beginnings of the Christian movement, Jesus was able to take the worst of sinners and make new people out of them. He took the prostitute Mary Magdalene and gave her new life. He met the Samaritan divorcee who had already gone through five husbands, and now had a "live-in," and transformed her life. (John 4) He changed her so powerfully that she went out and brought her whole town to the Master. Instead of taking what she wanted from others, she began to share with others the new life she had found. Jesus also forgave Peter after he had denied his Lord, and He made this vacillating disciple a leader of the early church.

Without the help and renewing power of God, all of us are enslaved to the selfish desires inherent in our own personalities. For some it is sex, others must have alcohol, some must dominate others and always get their own way. Still others are weak, cowardly, and fearful. For all of us, in whatever condition we are entrapped, Jesus came to bring new life; the history of the Christian faith is the story of people who have found new life in Christ. His power to deliver us from every type of bondage in which we find ourselves is as life-changing today as it was when He lived in Galilee.

Helen arrived at church one Sunday morning, placed her two-year-old son in the nursery, and came in to worship. As a child, she had grown up in Sunday school. Her parents had been active participants in their church. But in her high school years, Helen started rebelling. There didn't seem to her to be enough fun and fellowship in her church and youth groups.

After graduation from high school, she started going with a boy who had "had it" with church. They grew to care for each other and began supplying each other's sexual desires. Before long Helen was pregnant. She wanted to marry James, but he did not want the responsibility of a child and left her. She had a long, lonely pregnancy, finding love and support only from her parents.

When her baby was about a year old, she met Tim. He was a warm, outgoing young man, but he had almost no contact with religion. As Helen and Tim grew to care very much for each other, she learned that he did not even know who his father was. Tim's mother was drunk the night she conceived him. She had been with several "lovers," and she really didn't know which one was the father of her child. After Tim was born, his mother worked whenever she was sober enough, which was only part time. Tim's best support was his grandmother, who also lived alone but was much more dependable than his mother.

By the time Tim and Helen met, he had been dating for several years. Dates usually meant sex. However, Helen had had one bitter experience with sex without commitment, so she didn't want any more. She knew her father and mother had some problems, but they had found help at their church. Helen had grown up in a secure, caring family, and now that was what she wanted for herself and her son. Similarly, Tim liked what he saw in Helen's family, more than anything he had ever experienced.

Tim and Helen had decided to get married about a year before Helen showed up at church. She continued attending church by herself for a month or two. Once or twice Tim came with her. Then one night Tim received a phone call from a man in the church who said that he and a friend would like to come to their home and get better acquainted. So Tim extended an invitation to them to visit him and his family.

When the guests arrived, they began a friendly conversation with Tim and Helen about their family and their work. Soon they began to share their own faith. Before they left that night, these guests had helped Tim and Helen find Jesus Christ as their Savior and Lord.

Many changes began taking place in the lives of Tim and Helen. They joined the church and became part of a small group Bible study. Their understanding of the Christian life and what it meant to love and care for one another began to increase. They were finding great joy and happiness with each other. Their problems with a permanent relationship were being solved. A lovely daughter came to bless their home.

More than ten years have passed since Tim and Helen invited Jesus Christ into their lives. They have faced many problems and have had several difficult economic crises. But their love for each other has steadily grown stronger. They are part of a group of believers, all of whom are growing together toward mature relationships. They also spend a lot of time helping other people. They are truly happy with each other, and God is meeting the needs of the whole family. Their children are growing up in the security of a happy, loving home.

Frances, too, grew up in a Christian family that attended church faithfully. She heard the teachings of the Holy Scriptures at both home and Sunday school. But for some reason, the principles proclaimed in the Bible did not always appeal to her.

Attractiveness and the warmth of an outgoing personality made Frances a very popular girl, and she always aroused the attention of both nice and not-so-nice young men. She finished high school, prepared for secretarial work, and soon found a good job in a small office. Before long she had a "steady" boyfriend.

Frances had many arguments with her parents over their wishes that she marry a sincere Christian. Jim had no interest in church or the Christian faith, but he made a good living and was thoughtful of her, so what else mattered? She rejected the New Testament teaching that a Christian should marry a person of like faith and commitment to Jesus Christ. When she discovered that she was pregnant, she and Jim decided to elope and get married.

Since Frances had grown up in a church home, she had always wanted to be a wife and mother, so she was thrilled that her lifelong dream was about to be fulfilled. Jim, on the other hand, was not eager for the responsibilities of fatherhood. He and Frances were finding out that their goals in life were quite different. Their arguments and quarrels steadily increased.

Soon after baby Judy arrived, Jim discovered that he was into far more obligations than he wanted. He liked the simple life where he could have sexual excitement without commitment or responsibility. So when Judy was about six months old, Jim left her and Frances for his former lifestyle.

Desertion and the divorce which followed were a terrible blow to Frances. She did a lot of hard thinking. Finally, she found a job and her mother agreed to take care of Judy while she worked. She could cope with life financially, but her loneliness and hunger for intimacy were uncontrollable. Again, she began dating men who were attracted to her warm personality.

Dating nearly always meant sex, so she gradually developed a lifestyle of sexual freedom. Of course, her conscience bothered her because she continued to go to church with her parents. But she rationalized that we were living in a new age and Biblical guidelines no longer applied. Besides, "everyone" her age was doing it, and she wanted to be part of her generation.

About this time Frances met Carl and grew to be very fond of him. Carl was different from Jim in that he wanted children, but he was like Jim in his dislike for religion. This bothered Frances, but Carl was very warm and obviously loved her, and he and Judy were like father and daughter. Frances reasoned that she was older now and had developed better skills for living with men. And she was sure that, in time, Carl would go to church with her.

Thus, Frances and Carl were married and bought a nice home. Life went well for a while, and they decided to have a child to bless their marriage. When Gary was born, both his parents were thrilled. This family was basically a happy one. There were arguments now and then because both Carl and Frances were very aggressive. Through the rough times, Frances remained sure that time would smooth out the rough spots, but she failed to notice that Carl was showing strain and slow-ly lowering his level of affection for her.

The decay in the warmth that Carl and Frances had experienced during their first year of marriage was very gradual at first, but it was having a powerful effect on Carl because he couldn't stand conflict. After a few months, he became attracted to a very beautiful woman where he worked. A relationship developed which was satisfying to Carl sexually, and as a bonus, this new friend was not aggressive. Whatever Carl wanted to do seemed to please her. When Frances became suspicious, she and Carl had a violent argu-ment which ended with Carl announcing that he was all through and wanted out of the marriage. Apologies and pleadings by Frances did no good; Carl got his divorce.

A shattered Frances now faced the task of making a home for two children all by herself. However, she accepted this challenge with determination. She got a job that enabled her to keep her house and provide for her children, but the loneliness was devastating. She loved being with her children but longed for adult companionship.

A contributing factor to Frances' feeling of isolation was her lack of any real friendship with women her age. The married ones did not welcome her because she was too attractive to men. Yet she usually disliked those, like herself, who were divorced, because they were often aggressive with very negative attitudes. So these were lonely years in which she longed for inti-macy but could never seem to find it. It was a miser-able, lonely, disappointing and frustrating life. She knew there had to be something better because she had grown up in a stable Christian home.

When her children were half-way through elemen-tary school, Frances met a man at the plant where she worked who became interested in her. She was especially pleased because he was a Christian.

Though he belonged to a different church than hers, they found that they had much in common. Dale had high standards, and though he had never married, he believed that marriage was a lifelong covenant between a man, a woman, and the God who had created them. He knew that when he found the right person, he would be married in the church and have a Christian home.

About this time Frances decided to leave her parents' denomination. She began attending a new church filled with many young families. She was happier in this new Christian fellowship than she had ever been in her life. Soon Dale began going with her and her children. After a few weeks he decided that he too liked the new church. Before long, Dale and Frances became engaged and started making plans for a lovely wedding.

When they spoke to the minister about the possibility of being married in the sanctuary, he explained that he only married people after two or more sessions of pre-marriage counseling. During this counseling, Frances was amazed to discover that her aggressiveness and determination to always get her way made it difficult for any man to live with her for a long period of time. She resolved that with God's help, she would make some changes in her life. At this time, she came to a new understanding and respect for God's plan for sex in the sacred bond of marriage. This was a time when many things were changing for Frances, most important of which was a new commitment to God and his Holy Word.

When Dale and Frances were married in an impressive church wedding, it was really the beginning of a new life for both of them. They became part of a Bible study group which helped them apply the teachings of Jesus to their life situations, and they made many new friends who encouraged them in their maturing growth.

A little over a year later their son was born. Pat was a happy, eager, intelligent child who has grown into a fine man, now married with a family of his own. And what about Judy and Gary, the children born into a family where, in each instance, Frances had married one of her lovers? Judy married her first lover and had two children by him before they split up because her husband had found a new lover. And Judy, like her mother before her, is trying to support her family as a single parent. Her half-brother, Gary, now in his mid-forties, has never married. For him, family relationships have always seemed to be too tenuous and painful.

As for Dale and Frances, not only their companionship with each other, but all of life has grown more precious to them. They are maturing in a beautiful relationship and have now celebrated their twenty-fifth wedding anniversary. They have both reaped the rich rewards that come from following God's plan for lifelong fulfillment and intimacy in marriage.

Nobody is hopeless. There are no impossible situations where God is concerned. God is still able to meet us where we are and help us grow into mature, caring persons. What God has done, and is still doing, for Tim and Helen and Frances and Dale, he can also do for you and for me. All he needs is our cooperation. Our desire to change is the key to new life.

Steps to a Changed Life

The steps we need to take to break the enticement of sex with any willing person are very similar to the steps necessary to break any powerful addiction. The book, *Alcoholics Anonymous*, which is used by both drug and alcohol addicts, has twelve steps listed, on page 59 of the third edition, that will be helpful.

In my own experience of assisting people in change and growth, I have found the following steps essential.

First, we must recognize clearly that our past sexual behavior is against God's creative plan. We need to admit this to ourselves and one other human being. Along with this admission, we need to recognize the magnetic force of our past behavior and our inability to change it by our own efforts. It cannot be changed without our effort, but we will require additional help to support our growing determination to chart a new course.

Second, we need to recognize, in God and in his plan for human sexuality, the lifestyle that we want more than anything else in life. We must come to believe that God loves us in spite of our past and wants to help us become new persons. He will hear our prayer when we humbly ask him to forgive our past and help us to become the person he wants us to be.

Third, most will need human help in making this change. Your pastor or a Christian friend who is well grounded in the faith can answer many of your questions and assist you in finding the help which God wants to give you.

Finally, you will need the support of a Christian group or several Christian friends in a persistent study of the Bible, learning to apply its teachings to your life on a continuing and growing basis.

We Americans tend to be individualists. However, we do need each other. Jesus knew what he was doing when he chose twelve disciples to be with him. From him they learned how to meet life's problems and challenges. After Jesus was no longer with them in bodily form, they helped one another. Together they grew in their ability to be open to the guidance of the Holy Spirit and to meet the challenges they faced each day. You and I have this same need for each other's help and support. As we seek God's guidance together, we all grow in our ability to fulfill God's plan for us and to assist others in their upward journey.

The task of changing a long-standing way of life is not easy. You will probably find it the most difficult task you have ever undertaken. Remember, it is also the most rewarding. It may help you to recall that Jesus said, "Those who are well have no need of a physician, but those who are sick; I have not come to call the righteous, but sinners to repentance." (Luke 5:31-32) In other words, he did not come to help people who already had it made, or thought they did. He came to help us break the clutches of old habits and begin new ways of living. He is waiting now to forgive your past and empower you to live a life of caring fidelity. The choice is up to you.

CHAPTER ELEVEN

Teaching Children About God's Gift of Sexuality

I am including this final chapter to offer parents of young children a Christian philosophical foundation to which they can add their own biological teaching of human sexuality.

The Foundation for Teaching Human Sexuality

We live in a time when most parents are greatly concerned about the sex education their children are getting. Our era is especially difficult for those who want their children to have Christian values. Many parents do not feel qualified to do the job themselves. However, they are or should be the most natural sources for children to look to.

Nevertheless, many parents are embarrassed to talk to their own children about human sexuality. They feel very self-conscious and are afraid children will ask questions they are not prepared to answer. Hence, there is great confusion on the point of who should teach children, as well as what should be taught and at which ages.

Few parents want to do nothing and let nature take its course. But some think that the public school should undertake the task of sex education for all children, while many Christian parents oppose the school's teaching such a subject because the school is not allowed to give the Christian values they want their children to have.

Both school and counseling agencies, such as Planned Parenthood, are prepared to give good courses in human sexual biology. They do an excellent job of teaching proper terms for all parts of the reproductive system. They carefully explain what causes pregnancy, through the union of sperm and ovum, and how to prevent it. They also teach their students how to minimize venereal infections and where to go if one is contracted. However, most such agencies do not present Judeo-Christian moral values. They teach the wrongness of bringing an unwanted child into the world but are usually blind to the addictive power of promiscuous sex and unaware of its destructive force in the family.

Some parents will run into problems similar to those experienced by a family I knew. Their son was an "A" student, well advanced in scouting and active in his church. At age fifteen he got a crush on a fourteen-year-old girl. He suddenly began getting incomplete and failing marks at school. He dropped out of both scouts and church. The school counselor tried to work with the boy, his girlfriend, and the parents to bring some order back into the boy's life at school and at home.

The boy's parents were disturbed because sex with the girl had taken over his life so completely that he could accomplish nothing else, either at school or at home. When the parents expressed their concern over the problem and felt that their son's sexual behavior had to be changed, the counselor gave no help. She said to the parents, "What do you want him to do, stand in the corner and masturbate?"

This psychologist could see nothing wrong with daily sexual intercourse between a fifteen-year-old boy and a fourteen-year-old girl, so long as the girl stayed on the pill. Never mind that neither could make a living; ignore the fact that both were failing in school. That was a problem for parents and teachers. I wish this was an extreme case, but it is more representative of non-Christian attitudes toward human sexuality than most of us like to admit.

For parents who want the best training in human sexuality for themselves and their children, they must learn to rely on their church, and especially on the teachings of the Bible. In order to reach this goal, most will need help.

In this book my purpose is to provide you with resources for a Christian view of human sexuality. It is not my purpose to teach biology. Your gynecologist or general practitioner can do a much better job in this area. What I do want to provide is a Biblical understanding of sex.

Reverence for Marriage

As a foundation for understanding human sexuality, I want to use a scripture referred to in chapter five. I am choosing a passage from Hebrews because this is a general letter written by a leader of the early church to all Christians. He says: "Marriage is honorable; let us all keep it so, and the marriage-bond inviolate; for God's judgment will fall on fornicators and adulterers." (Heb. 13:4 NEB)

Commenting on this passage, Dr. J.Harry Cotton says:

> To hold marriage in honor is psychologically the best antidote for immorality of all kinds. Let growing children be given instruction in terms of marriage, the home that will one day be theirs, the love that they will want to hold sacred, and the children that will be given to them. *That is the core of all sound sex education.* It is also the best defense against defilement of the marriage bed.[1] (italics added)

---

[1]Nolan B. Harmon, *The Interpreter's Bible*, 12 Vols. (New York: Abingdon, 1955), Vol. 11, p. 753.

God is the source of all love. Through the gift of his son, Jesus Christ, he has shown us how to love and forgive those who do selfish and evil things which hurt us and others. Paul said, "God shows his love to us in that, while we were yet sinners, Christ died for us." (Rom. 5:8 RSV) In other words, God loved us not because we were so wonderful and irresistible that he couldn't help being attracted to us. He loved and loves us because we are his children, and even though we are selfish and rebellious, he still reaches out to us with caring love and protection. Through his forgiveness we become new, caring persons who learn to love others with the kind of love which we have experienced in God.

In marriage, we are still humans and therefore sinners. We must make the kind of commitment toward each other that God has made toward us. We should get married knowing that both we and our mates are sinners, as well as lovers, and, potentially, saints. In marriage we covenant with our mate to love and cherish him/her, to forgive their sins, and to be humble enough to admit our sins and seek our partner's forgiveness.

Finally, our children must learn that in the marriage covenant, we commit ourselves to love and redeem this imperfect person to whom we are married, just as we want him/her to help redeem us by forgiving our sins. This is not easy, but we know that Christ bore this cross for us, and we should bear it for each other. We believe that only as we bear our cross with patience will we develop the kind of character we find in Christ, which is the goal toward which all humanity is yearning.

This and nothing less than this is what it means to hold marriage in honor. If we run because we and our mate are having some difficulties, two results occur.

First, we are not following the Christ, who went all the way to the cross for our sins and did not turn back. Second, we are not developing the kind of character that bears all things and continues to grow in Christ. However, in giving this strong support to marriage as God intended it to be, I do not mean to say that any person must accept prolonged violence, abuse, or infidelity on the part of a spouse. Persons whose response to marital difficulties is violence or infidelity and who refuse to seek help to change their unacceptable behavior cannot expect to have durable marriages.

To exalt the home and family and make it a precious place for each member is the foundation for training in all relationships of which the sexual is one of the most important. If home is a wonderful place for the children, they naturally look forward with eagerness to the time when they will be fathers or mothers with families of their own. For instance, little girls start playing with dolls whom they can mother, while boys try to imitate their father.

When this kind of foundation has been carefully laid during their first years, elementary-age children are ready to begin understanding human sexuality by the time they reach grades four to six. However, it is important that this teaching be given them in terms of the mate they will one day choose and the home that will be theirs. Children can grasp the meaning of sex and family. Moreover, if the home that produced them has provided a sanctuary for them and their parents, that is the kind of home they will want for themselves. Children can and do exercise great discipline in reaching goals that are both clear and important to them.

I remember well my own sexual training. My parents clearly loved each other. My father had only a third-grade education, but he was a hard worker and a great reader, though I think he felt handicapped in teaching. Mother, who had a high school diploma, did most of the sexual training for my sister and me. She started early in my pre-school days talking with me first about flowers and how wonderfully God had planned for them to reproduce themselves. I remember counting the stamens and anthers and observing the pistils of many different flowers. Mother carefully explained the function of each. We found butterfly eggs, watched them hatch into caterpillars, eat and grow, spin into cocoons, and finally burst forth as butterflies.

We found birds' nests. Sometimes we watched in awe as the birds built their nests, father bird and mother bird mating, and checked the nests day by day as eggs were laid. Then we observed them during the incubation period while mother bird brooded the eggs. Sometimes we were lucky enough to hear the first squeaking voices of newly hatched birds and to see the babies before their eyes were open.

We went through the whole process with our female cat. We heard males fighting each other at night for the right to become our kitty's mate. We watched as our cat's abdomen filled out. Finally, there was the excitement of new baby kittens.

As I grew older, mother proceeded through insects and birds to mammals and finally humans. All the way she made reproduction a fascinating, beautiful plan made by our Creator. In her mind, there was never anything dirty about sex. It was a wonderful, holy, exciting part of our Creator's plan for continuing life in his great universe.

In our pre-puberty days, my sister and I were carefully coached and prepared for changes about to take place in our bodies. I was expecting my first nocturnal semenal emission before it took place. When it happened, I was thrilled to be growing up. My sister looked forward with eagerness to her first menstruation. These changes in us were made part of the whole of life. Our Creator had a plan for everything he had made; His plan was always to be eagerly sought as the best and most wonderful that life could provide.

As my sister and I grew older, mother made it clear that sex could be used in the wrong way and bring suffering to those involved and all who loved them. However, that did not mean that sex was shameful. It was a wonderful part of God's plan, but it was always to be used in the holy, divinely planned relationship between husband and wife.

We grew up knowing from the depths of our being that sex was to be revered and respected as a precious gift from the hand of God. We never wanted to use it in any other way, and we expected to find our joy and fulfillment through it after we were married. Thus, we knew that sex was planned as a holy tryst between husband and wife, bringing both physical and spiritual fulfillment.

My wife, Anna, and I found sex to be a powerful uniting force in our lives as we went through the stages of pregnancy, birth, nurturing of children, and finally maturing love, with just the two of us again, after the children were grown and in homes of their own.

This Foundation Works

A friend of mine who read an early version of this manuscript asked me to include a section about my own temptations to have sex with beautiful girls that I dated before I was married to Anna. I have thought about this request for the past four months, and I honestly cannot remember any real temptation of this sort. This may seem very strange, and I'm sure that some will feel that I have blocked off my true emotions. Of course, both as an adolescent and a young man, I experienced feelings of sexual stimulation and excitement when in the presence of an attractive girl or young woman. But instead of wanting to go to bed with her immediately, these feelings only made me more eager for marriage and increased my desire to find the right mate. For her, I was saving my full expression of masculine love.

I'm sure that many will understand what I am saying because they have had similar experiences. I think my parents set such a fine example and did such a good job with our sexual education, that for both my sister and me, sex outside of marriage was never an option. It was something I never toyed with at any time. Beginning in my late teens, I began serious dating and was eager to find a wife, but I never wanted a woman's body until she and I were committed to each other in marriage.

Marriage was the goal toward which I had been building my hopes and dreams ever since childhood. I was not prevented from having sex with an attractive girl by fear of responsibility or fear of getting a girl pregnant. Rather, I was beckoned on toward marriage. The sheer awe and wonder of life as God had planned it for all his children was calling me. I believed marriage to be the fulfillment of God's plan and that it would bring the most joy, pleasure, and satisfaction I could find in life. This was the ultimate, and I pressed on to reach this goal, rejecting all thoughts and action which led to lesser and more temporary pleasures.

In my search for a mate, I always dated girls who had goals similar to mine. If I got a date with a girl who was basically self-seeking and looking for immediate pleasure, I broke off the relationship after one or two dates. The girls I dated over longer periods were those who had Christian values and goals.

Eventually, Anna and I found each other. We are both grateful that our parents helped us understand the real meaning of life by being loving, caring persons. They established the kind of homes where God was loved and life was filled with learning, joy, and inspiration for each member of the family. Consequently, a deep reverence for life and for the process by which persons are created began early in our lives. Then the divine plan for sex became clearer and more fulfilling as we gained experience and understanding. We are both thankful for the richly rewarding life which it has brought to us.

You Can Trust This Plan

What our parents did for my sister and me, I'm sure most parents can do for their own children, although it takes some time and careful preparation. Still, most of us miss the boat by not starting soon enough. If we begin when our children are small and full of wonder and make it fun for them to learn many things from us, we have a good start. If we start with the thrill of life in germinating seeds when the child is three or four, we lay a good foundation. If our child learns that we know wonderful, fascinating things about life and how God planned for every creature—if he is aware of the wonder and awe in our lives—he will develop these qualities in his life.

Children who learn exciting, thrilling, and fun things about plant and animal life from their parents will want to discover what their parents know about human life. If we have taken the time to make the simple forms of God's creation exciting for children, they will also ask us about the more complex forms.

If reproduction in plants was an exciting event, then reproduction in animals is even more wonderful. If we have an open eagerness to share these areas with our children, they will be eager to find out what we have learned about human sexuality.

I realize that this may make some of you parents feel sad. You love your children, but they are now ten or twelve, or even in their teens, and you did not start discussing this topic when they were little. You are saying, "What can we do? We missed the boat."

I understand your feeling because I wish I had learned all that this recent research has taught me before our children reached puberty, but I didn't. I tried as best I could with what I knew, which was somewhat inadequate. None of us can go back and re-do the past, but we can start where we are now.

Begin now, whatever the age of your children. Set an example of love and caring between yourself and your spouse. Always relate sexual teaching to marriage and children. As we have seen, within marriage, sex serves other purposes than creating children. But when sex is totally separated from procreation and becomes only a fun thing to be expressed for the thrill of the moment, it begins to destroy us, because we are misusing it.

Finally, human sexuality, both ours and our children's, is a beautiful gift, straight from the mind and heart of our Creator. It was given to assist committed mates in developing closeness and relational maturity. It helps us in understanding, loving, and sharing the most intimate parts of our being with our mate. It is ours to use in life-long bliss with our spouse as we both grow into our Creator's dream. It is ours to pass on to our children with the same holy reverence and joy with which we received it from God.

Biblical References To Sexual Teaching And Behavior

1. Creation account of male and female — Gen. 1:27-28
2. Birth of first child Gen. 4:1
3. Sarai's solution to barrenness — Gen. 16:1-6
4. The Abrahamic covenant and circumcision — Gen. 17:1-21
5. Sodomites attempt homosexual rape — Gen. 19:1-11
6. Lot's daughters commit incest with him — Gen. 19:30-38
7. Isaac & Rebecca seen making love — Gen. 26:8
8. Jacob's two wives and their maids — Gen. 30:1-24
9. Shechem rapes DinahGen. 34:1-31
10. Onan uses birth control — Gen. 38:8-11
11. Tamar seduces JudahGen. 38:12-26
12. Joseph and Potiphar's wife — Gen. 39:6-23
13. Adultery forbidden in Israel — Ex. 20:14 / Deut. 5:18
14. A man must pay father for seduced daughter — Ex. 22:16-17
15. Death penalty for copulating with animals — Ex. 22:19 / Lev. 18:23 / Deut. 27:21
16. Israelites make a golden calf (idol worship). A fertility cult was probably involved. See TEV — Ex. 32:6
17. Uncleanness of semen emission — Lev. 15:16, 22:4 / Deut. 23:10-11
18. Menstrual uncleanness — Lev. 15:19-30

19. Uncleanness at childbirth   Lev. 12:1-8

20. Israel's sexual behavior is always to be
    different from Gentiles. Specifically
    forbids adultery, homosexual behavior,   Lev. 18:1-30;
    and copulating with an animal.   20:23

21. Guilt and cleansing for adultery.   Lev. 19:20-22

22. A man shall not make his daughter a
    harlot.   Lev. 19:29

23. Laws against adultery, incest, homosexual
    behavior, and copulation with animals.   Lev. 20:10-21

24. High marriage standards for priests.   Lev. 21:7-9

25. Israelites have sexual relations with
    Moabite women, worship Baal, and are
    punished.   Num. 25:1-18

26. Early Hebrew laws of virginity, rape, and
    adultery.   Deut. 22:13-30

27. Cult prostitutes, both male and female,
    prohibited.   Deut. 23:17-18

28. Laws governing divorce and remarriage.   Deut. 24:1-4

29. Curse pronounced on those who commit
    incest or copulate with an animal.   Deut. 27:20-23

30. Rape at Gibeah.   Jud. 19:1-30

31. David's adultery with Bathsheba   II Sam. 11-12

32. Amnon rapes Tamar.   II Sam. 13:1-33

33. Absalom violates David's concubines.   II Sam. 16:20-23

34. Solomon has 700 wives and 300
    concubines.   I Kings 11:3

35. Warnings against a loose woman.	Prov. 5:3-20
36. Exhortation—be faithful to your wife.	Prov. 5:18-19
37. Warnings about harlots and adulteresses.	Prov. 6:24-33
38. Warnings about seductive women.	Prov. 7:5-27
39. An adulteress denies her sin.	Prov. 30:20
40. Praise of a good wife.	Prov. 31:10-29
41. A king delights in concubines.	Ecc. 2:8
42. Lovers describe physically attractive lovers	Song of Soloman
43. Adultery—a sin that brings national ruin.	Eze. 33:26
44. Hosea most probably requires allegorical interpretation. Hosea believed he was commanded by God to marry a harlot and raise children by her. He used this situation with an unfaithful wife to point out the infidelity of Israel to God. Most of the book follows this theme.	Hosea
45. Father and son patronizing the same prostitute profanes God's name.	Amos 2:7
46. The Lord hates divorce	Mal. 2:13-16
47. The virgin birth. Joseph suspects Mary of infidelity, plans to divorce her until God intervenes.	Matt. 1:18-21 Luke 1:26-35
48. Jesus warns against lust which leads to adultery.	Matt. 5:27-30
49. Jesus rejects divorce except for infidelity.	Matt. 5:31-32
50. Jesus says God planned for marriage to last until death. Moses permitted divorce because of the hardness of peoples' hearts.	Matt. 19:3-9 Mark 10:2-12 Luke 16:18

51. Jesus says that fornication, adultery,
    murder, theft, ruthless greed, and other   Mark 7:21-23
    such practices make one unclean.   Matt. 15:15-20

52. Jesus talks with a Samaritan woman
    who had had five husbands and a live-in.   John 4:7-42

53. Jesus deals with the woman caught in
    adultery.   John 8:1-11

54. The Jerusalem Conference. Gentile
    converts required to abstain from
    fornication (sexual immorality).   Acts 15:19-29

55. Because people do not honor God, they
    fall under the control of lust and passion
    and end up in all manner of wickedness,
    including homosexual perversion.   Rom. 1:24-32

56. A person may remarry after the death of   Rom. 7:1-3
    a mate.   I Cor. 7:39-40

57. Paul is shocked by a report of sexual
    immorality between a man and his step-   I Cor. 5:1-5;
    mother at Corinth.   9-11

58. The unrighteous will not inherit God's
    Kingdom. The unrighteous include those
    guilty of sexual immorality and other sins.   I Cor. 6:9-11

59. The human body is not meant for sexual
    immorality.   I Cor. 6:13-20

60. Advice for husbands and wives, the
    unmarried and widows.   I Cor. 7:1-38

61. Christians should only marry Christians   I Cor. 7:39
                                                     II Cor. 6:14-18
62. Christians must not be guilty of sexual
    immorality.   I Cor. 10:8

63. Paul fears that if he visits Corinth again he
    may find some who have not repented of the
    sexual immorality they previously practiced.   II Cor. 12:21

64. The Galatian and Ephesian Christians are
    warned that those who practice sexual
    immorality and other sins will not inherit   Gal. 5:19-21
    the Kingdom of God.   Eph. 5:3-5

65. Christians advised to put to death what is
    earthly in them—sexual immorality,
    idolatry, covetousness.   Col. 3:5-10

66. Thessalonians are told that the will of God
    requires abstention from fornication or
    sexual immorality.   I Thess. 4:1-8

67. Paul tells Timothy that the law is not
    necessary for good people, but to restrain
    the lawless, including sexually immoral.   I Tim. 1:8-11

68. All should hold marriage in honor. God
    will judge fornicators and adulterers.   Heb. 13:4

69. Adultery and murder are equated as
    violations of God's law.   James 2:11

70. The Christian is to leave in the past
    Gentile behavior like sexual lust, passions,
    drunkenness.   I Pet. 4:3

71. Peter condemns false prophets in the   II Pet. 2:1-3;
    church who have eyes full of sexual lust.   12-14

72. Jude is concerned about false Christians
    who have wormed their way into the church
    and whose lives are filled with sexual lust.   Jude 4-7

73. The living Christ writes letters to seven Asian
    churches. Three of these churches had
    problems with those wanting to adopt   Rev. 2:6;
    loose sexual behavior.   14-16; 20-22

< B I B L I O G R A P H Y >

Alcoholics Anonymous, *Alcoholics Anonymous. 3rd ed.*, New York: Alcoholics Anonymous World Services, Inc., 1976.

Barclay, William, ed. *The Gospel of Luke.* Philadelphia: Westminster Press, 1956.

————. *The Gospel of Matthew*, Rev. Ed. Philadelphia: Westminster, 1975. Vol. 1.

————. "The Letters and the Revelation,"*The New Testament, a New Translation*, Vol. 2. London/New York: Collins Press, 1969.

————. *The Letters to James and Peter.* Philadelphia: Westminster, 1956.

————. *The Letter to the Romans.* Rev. Ed. Philadelphia: Westminster, 1975.

————. *The Letters to the Corinthians.* Philadelphia: Westminster, 1956.

————. *The Revelation of John.* Philadelphia: Westminster, 1960. Vol. 1.

The Good News Bible. Nashville: Broadman, 1976.

Harmon, Nolan B., ed. *The Interpreter's Bible.* 12 Vols. New York: Abingdon, 1953. Vol. 2.

————. *The Interpreter's Bible.* 12 Vols. New York: Abingdon, 1955. Vol. 11.

————.*The Interpreter's Bible.* 12 Vols. New York: Abingdon, 1957. Vol. 12.

The Holy Bible. Revised Standard Version (RSV). Philadelphia: A.J. Holman Co., 1962.

International Bible Society. *Holy Bible.* New International Version (NEB). Grand Rapids: Zondervan, 1983.

Laymon, Charles M., ed. *The Interpreter's One-Volume Commentary.* New York: Abingdon, 1971.

The New English Bible with the Apocrypha(NEB). London: Oxford University Press/Cambridge University Press, 1970.